THE SECOND VOICE

DEALING WITH THE ENEMY AND HIS STRATEGIES

Cynthia McKnight

THE SECOND VOICE:
DEALING WITH THE ENEMY AND HIS STRATEGIES

by Cynthia McKnight

Printed in the United States of America
Copyright © September 2019

ISBN: 978-1-64550-509-9

Unless otherwise indicated, Bible quotations are taken from the King James Version, New Living Translation, or the New International Version of the Bible unless otherwise stated.

AUTHOR'S BIO

The multifaceted creative, Cynthia McKnight is a writer, producer, counselor, mentor, entrepreneur, trainer, and speaker. For the past twenty years, Cynthia has been the CEO of *Eyes on You Productions and Consulting Company.* Beyond the realm of the arts, Cynthia has owned multiple businesses during her tenure as an entrepreneur. The most recent business is a family-owned seafood business, called *"Jus' Shrimp."* Cynthia is a sought

after producer of Christian stage plays, short films, and inspired arts productions. Her production company, *Eyes on You Productions* uses the arts as a platform to promote positive and inspiring messages. Her greatest desire is to see people come to a saving knowledge of Jesus Christ, submit their lives to His teachings so that their lives are transformed. To that end, Cynthia has also reached over 10,000 women through her teaching of the Word.

DEDICATION

In memory of the most amazing, and wonderful father; my loving Dad, James T. Fitzgerald. I will always be Daddy's little girl!

ACKNOWLEDGEMENTS

To my Lord and Savior Jesus Christ, and to the Holy Spirit who has given me the wisdom, guidance, and direction to produce this book for the advancement of the kingdom. I am eternally grateful.

To the greatest husband to grace the face of this earth, Warren C. McKnight, Sr., I thank you for your continuous love and support in the writing of this book.

To my wonderful children who are the love of my life; Latoya McKnight Hall, Lateesha McKnight, Warren "Chris" McKnight, and Latayana McKnight

TABLE OF CONTENTS

OVERVIEW

PART ONE
THE PLOT

PART TWO
THE PRESCRIPTION

PART THREE
THE PRIZE

INTRODUCTION

<u>THE</u> VOICE

Today, there are three primary voices in the world – God's voice, Satan's voice, and your voice. However, in the beginning that was not the case. In the beginning, there was only one voice... <u>THE</u> Voice... GOD's Voice!

GOD'S UNITED VOICE
God's voice is a united voice. His voice is the voice of the Trinity. The Trinity – Father, Son and Holy Spirit – all spoke with the same voice. They were in perfect unity at all times, in all matters so that there were no conflicts, no disagreements... ever!

GOD'S CREATIVE VOICE
God's united voice was manifested in creation. When the Holy Spirit moved over the surface of the waters and saw that the earth was formless and empty and that darkness was everywhere, the Trinity spoke with one united voice, *"Let there be..."* (Gen 1:2-3) and in six days created the heavens and the earth.

GOD'S POWERFUL VOICE
Creation also testifies to the power of God's voice. By simply speaking, God took nothing and created everything. That is power... pure, unadulterated POWER!!!

To make sure that the power of His voice is clearly understood, God made this declaration through the prophet Isaiah.

My word that goes out from my mouth will not return to me empty but will accomplish what I desire and achieve the purpose for which I sent it (Isaiah 55:11, NIV).

The power of God's voice is manifested by the fact that whatever He says will happen... happens! His powerful voice is creative. *Let there be*, and things came into existence. However, when necessary, His voice can also be destructive. The last book of the Bible, Revelation tells us what Jesus (God the Son), will do to His enemies. *Coming out of his mouth is a sharp sword with which to strike down the nations* (Rev 19:15) that have rejected Him and His offer of salvation. *They were **killed** with the sword coming out of the mouth of the rider on the white horse* (Rev 19:21). We know that this is not a literal sword, but the sword is symbolic of His Word (Eph. 6:17), His powerful voice that is able to create or destroy when He speaks.

GOD'S INSTRUCTIVE VOICE
In addition to being a united voice with power to create or destroy, God's voice is also instructive. After God made Adam and Eve, He gave them these instructions in Gen 1:28.

Rule over the fish in the sea and the birds in the sky and over every living creature that moves on the ground.

Since Adam was made in the image and likeness of God, he was made to use his voice and exercise authority over the area of his rulership – the earth. Therefore we see Adam using his voice to rule to exercise his dominion by naming the animals (Gen. 2:19-20). Adam acted in concert with God's instruction, so God gave Adam another instruction (Gen. 2:17). This time it was a prohibition, which carried with it consequences for disobedience.

You must not eat from the tree of the knowledge of good and evil, for when you eat from it you will certainly die.

After God proclaimed that it was not good for Adam to be alone, He made a helper suitable for him so that they could have dominion together, ruling together with one voice over the earth, just as the Trinity ruled together with one voice over the expansive universe. Assuming his rightful authority, Adam passed on God's instruction to Eve not to eat from the tree of the knowledge of good and evil. Eve heeded Adam's voice, which was in concert with God's voice. Everyone was on one accord and all was well.

THE SECOND VOICE

Then one day, unexpectedly, in the Garden of Eden, there was another voice, a second voice. It was Satan's voice speaking to Eve. But this voice had NO authority to speak to Eve. That was Adam's responsibility, but Adam's voice was <u>silent</u>. Not only was Satan speaking to Eve inappropriately, but he was also contradicting the voice of God, saying:

> You will <u>not</u> surely die for God knows that you will be <u>like</u>
> <u>God</u>, knowing good and evil (Gen 3:4-5).

Where was Adam's voice, exposing Satan's words as a lie by repeating what God said? Where was Adam's voice of authority over the Second Voice to rule over his home, banishing him from the Garden, and from influencing his wife? His voice was silent and so the Second Voice prevailed. Eve was deceived! She ate the fruit as Adam stood, silently, watching her disobey God's voice. To make matters worse, Adam also ate of the fruit, knowing that the consequence of this willful act of defiance was ***death***.

And so, from that day to this, we have all struggled with the Second Voice that contradicts what God says in his effort to get us to disobey God's voice. That is why I wrote this book. It is a guide that you can use:
1. *to identify* the Second Voice (Satan's voice), and the devices he uses to get us to doubt, deny and disobey God's voice
2. *to develop strategies* to use to turn up the volume on God's voice, diminish the confusing noise from the Second Voice, and use the authority we have to live the abundant life

PROLOGUE

A LETTER FROM ADAM AND EVE
Words of Wisdom From the First Parents

To my beloved daughters from Mother Eve:

Adam is going to write to the men, but I wanted to talk from my heart to all of my daughters:

First, I would like to apologize for being so gullible and causing you to have pain during childbirth. I know I have been criticized over the years for eating the forbidden fruit and then getting Adam to eat it. At the time, I felt that I was simply sharing with Adam so that both of us would become MORE like God by gaining the knowledge of good and evil. The problem was, I bought Satan's lie that God was keeping something beneficial from us, and that He wanted to scare us by saying we would die if we ate the fruit.

You are right. I should have known better. We were in such an intimate relationship with God, I should have known better. Every day God came to fellowship with us the Garden. We took long walks and talked with God about everything you could imagine. I enjoyed those times so much, and so did Adam. God's love for us was quite obvious. In fact, He told us every day how much He loved us and how we were the apple of His eye, greatly loved and so precious to Him. But after a while, we both began to take His love for granted.

LESSONS LEARNED: If I knew then what I know now, I would have done things differently. So I would like to share with you a couple of lessons that I learned. You see, my daughters, I do not want you to make the same mistakes that I made.

Satan Is Devious – Run From Him:
Satan uses deception effectively by mixing a little truth with a big lie. Do not listen to him. You see, his only purpose is to steal from you God's blessings, to kill and destroy all that God has planned and purposed for you. Reject Satan's lie! Submit to God's voice!

God Is Love – Run To Him:
God loves you! I know that seems basic, but it is important to keep this uppermost in your mind and heart. Because God loves you supremely, He only has the best for you; therefore, you can trust Him. When God gives you a command, it is for your good. Never doubt that! Though you may not understand why, if you remember that God loves you then you will obey His voice and receive His blessing instead of His judgment.

Women Have Influence – Use It For Good:
Women have great influence, especially over their husbands. Satan used me to disobey God, and then I used my influence to get Adam to disobey God as well. Do not do that! Use the influential power that you have for good, and not evil. Use your influence to help and not to hinder God's plan and purpose. If you follow my advice, you and your family will be able to live the abundant life that God has purposed for you.
Blessings always, Mother Eve

To my sons in the faith from Adam:

Eve spoke to the women so I just have a few words for the men. I will keep it short and to the point. Allow me to share two thoughts – words of wisdom that I learned from the disaster that occurred in the Garden of Eden.

Assume Your Authority:
When God created me, it was in His likeness and image. And *like* Him, He gave me the authority to rule over the earth and the animals. When the serpent started talking to my wife I did not use my God-given authority to stop the serpent from lying to my wife, and kick the serpent out of the Garden. Why? I really don't know. Maybe I wanted to hear what he had to say. But once he contradicted God's Word and said "*you shall* NOT *certainly die,*" that's when I should have stepped in. Instead, I foolishly remained silent. Men, do not do that. You are to study God's Word, know God's Word, and then speak that Word, especially to your wives, and particularly if someone is contradicting the truth. Speak up! Do not be silent!

Accept the Responsibility:
Another monumental mistake I made was to blame my wife for my failure. When God came to the Garden, he correctly called my name even though Eve ate first. I failed in my responsibility to protect my wife from danger and compounded the mistake by blaming her. Men, shoulder your responsibility like a man. If you are wrong, own up to it. Confess it to God, ask for forgiveness so that you can move forward and not stay stuck in your failure. As a matter of fact, when you blame others for your failure, it makes you appear to be weak. A strong, confident man will admit wrong, and try to correct it if at all possible.

I want you to know that I am praying that you will be all and do all that God has planned and purposed for your life.

Faithfully yours, your Father, Adam

PART ONE
THE PLOT

THE VOICE OF THE BIG "I"
The Origin of Pride

THE VOICE OF THE INTRUDER
Satan's Disguise

THE VOICES IN THE GARDEN
Satan's Success

THE VOICE OF THE ACCUSER
Satan's Strategy

THE SECOND VOICE IS...
The Voice of the Liar
The Voice of the Killer
The Voice of the Thief
The Voice of the Destroyer

OVERVIEW OF PART ONE
THE PLOT

Satan has a plot. It is an evil plot. His goal, his aim, his design and everything that he has planned is for your destruction. This means that there is a target on your back and Satan has you in his sights. Ever since he was kicked out of heaven and cast down to the earth, he has been in a rage. He hates God, but since he cannot defeat the Almighty, he goes after the next best target – the ones that God loves. Understand that he is merciless in his attacks and will use every trick in his arsenal to steal from you, kill you and destroy you. Therefore we are here to expose him. What made a beautiful archangel turn into a devil? What are his evil tactics? How do you recognize his voice, the Second Voice that is so skilled at the art of deception? To defeat your enemy, you have to know who he is, and you have to understand his strategies. That is exactly what you will discover in part one of this book – **THE PLOT**!

CHAPTER 1

THE VOICE OF THE BIG "I"
The Origin of Pride

There is a question that begs to be asked. Where did the Second Voice come from? Since in the beginning there was only one voice, God's united voice, where did the Second Voice come from? Surprisingly, the Second Voice originated in the most unlikely place of all... in heaven.

THE ARCHANGELS

God created angels to serve Him and worship Him continually. Among the innumerable host of angels are three special angels known as Archangels, which means the chief of the angels. The three archangels are Gabriel, Michael, and Lucifer. Each archangel was given a specific responsibility and had many angels under his authority. Gabriel, the chief messenger angel, was sent to deliver important messages to Daniel, the prophet (Dan. 9:21, 10:2-3), to Zechariah, the priest (Luke 1:19), and to Mary, the mother of Jesus (Luke 1:26-27). Michael is the chief warrior angel as seen in Revelation 12:7. *"Michael and his angels fought with the dragon and his angels"* (NKJV). Lucifer, the third archangel, who was in charge of leading worship of the one and only God, was created with beauty and splendor beyond measure. This is how he is described in Ezekiel 28:12-14 (NLT).

You were the model of perfection, full of wisdom and exquisite in beauty... Your clothing was adorned with every precious stone—red carnelian, pale-green peridot, white moonstone, blue-green beryl, onyx, green jasper, blue lapis lazuli, turquoise, and emerald—all beautifully crafted for you and set in the finest gold. They were given to you on the day you were created. I ordained and anointed you as the mighty angelic guardian. You had access to the holy mountain of God and walked among the stones of fire.

THE BIG "I"

That was Lucifer, magnificent, gorgeous beyond belief, created as the chief worshipper and musician. He was tasked to lead the angelic hosts in bowing down in worship, reverence and praise to the one who is worthy. But something happened to Lucifer. He was not satisfied with all that he was given, and used that very exalted position, given by God, to declare in his heart with such arrogance:

I will ascend to the heavens; I will raise my throne above the throne of God; I will sit enthroned on the mount of assembly... I will ascend above the tops of the clouds; I will make myself like the Most High (Isaiah 14:13-14).

That is the voice of pride, the voice of the Big "I". That is the origin of the Second Voice, which spoke against **THE Voice** who had appointed him to use his voice in worship. Now the Big "I" uses his voice to oppose the one who gave him his position in the first place.

And did you notice how many times he used the word "I". Five times he said, "I WILL." The five things his prideful heart desired to do, the Second Voice spoke out of his mouth:

1. To ascend to the place where God was
2. To dethrone God by raising his throne above God's throne
3. To sit in the exalted place that belongs to God
4. To ascend to the highest level possible
5. To make himself like the Most High God

He then used his voice to convince and deceive one third of the angels to rebel with him, to fight against God, to dethrone Him, and to assume God's exalted position. It is inconceivable to think that these angels, created beings, could actually believe that they could fight and win against the One who created them. It defies the obvious logic that the One who created you is GREATER than you are! And yet, humans do the same thing every single day.

Whenever we disobey God's voice that is revealed in His Word, we are opposing God. In essence, we are saying that I know better than God does, and will, therefore do things "my way" instead of God's way. That is the same sense of pride that was found in Lucifer, which caused him to rebel against the Most High God.

The best that Lucifer could *attempt* to do was to make himself "*like* the Most High." Even in his pride, he knew that he could not be *above* the Most High. After all, to be the MOST High, is to be the HIGHEST. Nothing and no one can supersede the Almighty. And so, the Most High dealt with this rebellion by using His voice of absolute authority to expel Lucifer and his rebellious followers out of heaven as explained in Ezekiel 28:15-17 (NLT).

> *You were blameless in your ways from the day you were created till wickedness was found in you... and you sinned. So I drove you in disgrace from the mount of God, and I expelled you from among the fiery stones. Your heart became proud on account of your beauty, and you corrupted your wisdom because of your splendor. So I threw you to the earth.*

In trying to get more than what he was already given, Lucifer and his followers lost the exalted positions they were given. There are always consequences to pride and rebellion. Therefore, in trying to get MORE than what was rightfully theirs, they lost their *place* in heaven, as well as the *position* of power and proximity to God that they had enjoyed.

But the loss was much more catastrophic than being expelled from heaven and enjoying the pleasure of being in the presence of God. The loss was so complete that their very nature changed. They no longer had a propensity to do good and obey God's voice. Instead, they were completely evil, opposing everything that is good and godly.

These angels became demons, and they have a new leader. Instead of obeying the voice of God, they now heed the commands of the Second Voice, the voice of Satan. Because of this drastic change in his nature, in what God had created Lucifer to be and to do, there was also a corresponding change in his name and his identity. No longer Lucifer, the one who is "*bringing light*," now he is Satan, the "*adversary*," the one who opposes. So Satan, the Second Voice, stands in opposition to God. But he cannot fight God and win, so he does the next best thing. Satan opposes the people God loves, the ones He created in His own image and likeness.

So now there are two voices competing for your attention, the Voice of God and the Second Voice, the prideful voice of the Big "I." The choice that each of us must make is the same choice that the angels had to make so very long ago… *which voice will you listen to*? The majority, two-thirds of the angels chose to heed God's voice, but one-third chose to follow the Second Voice and experienced great loss. The same is true for us today. Whenever we choose to listen to the voice of Satan instead of God's voice, we lose. We lose our joy, we lose our faith, we lose our peace, we lose the precious closeness of the presence of God in our lives. And guess what? Satan wins because we have chosen to obey him, and that is making him appear to be *like* God. His ultimate desire is to be worshipped *like* God. Do not allow your adversary to win in your life by obeying his voice, by focusing on self – your wants, your desires – above the voice of God. If you do, you will only lose the blessings God has for you, just *like* Lucifer lost all that God had given him.

24

CHAPTER 2

THE VOICE OF THE INTRUDER – PART 1
Satan's Motives

Intrusion is a hostile word! Merriam-Webster defines intrude as *"to put oneself deliberately into a place or situation where one is unwelcome or uninvited."* That is exactly what Satan did when he lost his place and position as the archangel of worship. Due to his prideful rebellion, his desire to exalt himself and take the position of the Most High God, he was quickly and violently expelled from heaven and cast down to the earth. In fact, Jesus describes it like this in Luke 10:18. *"I saw Satan fall like lightning from heaven."*

THE INTENTION OF THE INTRUDER
Having been cast down to the earth, **where did Satan go**? The intruder goes to the Garden of Eden. He crashed, uninvited into the home of Adam and Eve.

Eden – A Prepared Place: God is intentional…. always. And so from the beginning, God designed the earth specifically for the man and the woman with everything they needed to thrive. But then, God did something extra special. *"The Lord God planted a garden in Eden, and there he put the man he had formed"* (Gen. 2:8). That extra time and effort God spent preparing Eden was a display of the great love and care He had for them, just like proud parents preparing a special place for the arrival of their first child.

Eden – A Peaceful Place: Eden literally means *delight*. So the Garden of Eden God made is a *Garden of Delight* for this first couple. In this peaceful place, they were able to do all that God had destined for them. In this beautifully prepared home, they could be *"fruitful and multiply and fill the earth"* (Gen 1:28) with offspring so that God could shower His love on their descendants as well.

Eden – A Purposeful Place: Because God is intentional in everything He does, He declared His purpose for mankind before He created humans. *"Let us make man in mankind in our image, in our likeness so that they may rule over the fish in the sea and the birds in the sky, over the livestock and all the wild animals, over all the creatures that move along the ground"* (Gen. 1:26). That is God's stated purpose, for the man Adam and his helpmeet, Eve. They were to rule together over the earth *like* the way the Trinity (Father, Son, and Holy Spirit), ruled together over the universes. And Eden, this delightful, peaceful place, would be their headquarters, the place from which they would rule.

Eden – A Plentiful Place: In the Garden of Eden, God provided everything Adam and Eve would ever need. *"The Lord God made all kinds of trees grow out of the ground—trees that were pleasing to the eye and good for food. In the middle of the garden were the tree of life and the tree of the knowledge of good and evil. A river watering the garden flowed from Eden"* (Gen. 2:9-10). Everything they needed – provision, prosperity, peace – God provided in abundance.

Eden – A Prohibitive Place: The Garden had everything Adam could possibly want, but it came with one single prohibition. *"The Lord God commanded the <u>man</u>, "You are free to eat from any tree in the garden; but you must not eat from the tree of the knowledge of good and evil, for when you eat from it you will certainly die"*(Gen 2:16-17). Notice the command was given to Adam because Eve was not made until after Adam named all the animals and realized that none of them was suitable helper for him (Gen 2:20-22).

Eden – A Perfect Place: When God finished His creative work, He declared that it was very good (Gen. 1:31), in other words – perfect! That perfection included the brand-new home Adam and Eve lived in. The Garden of Eden was beautiful. It was plentiful and peaceful. It was purposeful and delightful. It was all they needed and all they could possibly want, freely given to them by the God who lovingly placed them together in a perfect place to exercise their God-given dominion and rule. How awesome!

THE ACTION OF THE INTRUDER

Having been cast down to the earth, **what does Satan _do_**? He not only goes directly to the home of Adam and Eve, he not only intrudes where he does not belong, but he enters their home in a disguise. Knowing that he is unwelcome, he comes in the form of a snake, masquerading as one of the animals so that his true identity remains concealed. This is a tactic that Satan still uses that is extremely effective. Satan will use other people, and often those closest to you to attack you. He will disguise himself in situations as he did with Job when he caused him to lose everything that Job cherished in one day (Job 1:13-19). Satan also used Job's wife to try to get him to curse God (Job 2:9). Be aware, Satan will also intrude into your life disguised as an angel of light according to 2 Corinthians 11:13-14. *"People such as false apostles, and deceitful workers masquerade as apostles of Christ. And no wonder, for Satan himself masquerades as an angel of light."* We must be wise and be on guard against the tools and tactics of the enemy to avoid being deceived like Eve.

THE MOTIVATION OF THE INTRUDER

Satan intrudes in the Garden with ulterior, evil motives to deceive. We know his motives are corrupt because he does not address the head. He does not go to the man, Adam. Instead, he circumvents proper protocol, defies the authority of the one who is in charge, disguises himself, and approaches the woman who he shrewdly detects as an easier target to convince to rebel against God.

CHAPTER 3

THE VOICE OF THE INTRUDER – PART 2
Satan's Attack

Having been cast down to the earth, having intruded into the Garden, masquerading as a serpent, **what does Satan _say_**? *"He said to the woman, "Did God really say, 'You must not eat from any tree in the garden'?"* When the intruder speaks, he launches a three-prong attack of doubt, denial, and deception.

VOICE OF DOUBT: The voice of the intruder is the voice of doubt. His words got Eve to question what it is that God said. *"Did God really say, 'You must **not** eat from **any** tree in the garden'?"* He starts by saying, Did God *really* say… He implies that God's command must be incredulous… could God *really* say THAT? He implies that you may have misunderstood what God *really* said. The Second Voice takes God's words, misquotes and twists it in order to cast doubt. Up to this point, God's word was a settled fact, but now, there is a consideration, a question about what God *really* said. Notice how Satan twists God's words, using the absolute terms… **not** and **any**. Did God really say you must **not** eat from **any** tree in the Garden, when God actually told Adam, *"You are **FREE** to eat from **any** tree in the garden"* (Gen 2:16a)? Satan causes us to doubt God's Word by questioning truth, by misstating truth, thereby making God's Word appear to be unreasonable.

1. Why can't I marry him just because he doesn't go to church? Being unequally yoked isn't that big of a deal if you love each other. Besides, he'll change once we get married.
2. What's wrong with sex before marriage? After all, you should try before you buy. That only makes good sense.
3. Forgive her? No way! You don't understand what she did to me! God could not expect me to forgive something as awful as that.
4. Be anxious for nothing? You don't understand! They are going to evict me and I have nowhere to go! That's fine for you to say, but I can't help being worried.

VOICE OF DENIAL: The voice of the intruder is also the voice of denial. When Satan raises doubt about the validity of what God told them about eating from any tree in the Garden, Eve responds with a partially inaccurate statement of what God said.

> *The woman said to the serpent, "We may eat fruit from the trees in the garden, but God did say, 'You must not eat fruit from the tree that is in the middle of the garden, and you must not touch it, or you will die'"* (Gen. 3:2-3).

Eve only got the first part of the statement correct. They were indeed free to eat fruit from the trees in the Garden. But then she falters when she declared what God actually said. *'You must not eat fruit from the tree that is in the middle of the garden.'* That was true according to Genesis 2:9b. *In the middle of the garden were the tree of life <u>and</u> the tree of the knowledge of good and evil.* Eve, there were actually **two** trees in the middle of the Garden so which tree are you referring to. You could eat from the Tree of Life, but NOT from the Tree of the Knowledge of Good and Evil. Eve needed to name the tree they were not to eat from. I know it may seem as if that is being picky, but we must be accurate with what God says. God is a precise God, and we must rightly divide (i.e. interpret) the Word of truth. We cannot afford to be fuzzy or unclear about declaring what God requires of us.

Eve is not only imprecise about which tree, but she also adds to what God said. *"and you must not **touch** it, or you will die."* God did not say anything about touching the fruit. Let's revisit EXACTLY what God said in Genesis 2:16-17.

> *You are **FREE** to eat from any tree in the garden, but you must not eat from the tree of the knowledge of good and evil, for when you **eat** from it you will **certainly die**.*"

What a mess! Eve not only added touching the fruit, but she left out the fact that God said, "You will *certainly* die." In other words, there is no shade of gray. Death will certainly result if you disobey.

The word *certainly* is important because it speaks to the extent of the death they would experience. In the Hebrew, it literally means, *"in dying you will die."* That is a reference to the three types of death they would experience – spiritual death, physical death, and eternal death. Death is simply defined as separation, therefore:

1. **Spiritual death** is to be spiritually separated from God.
2. **Physical death** occurs when the spirit separates from the body (absent from the body, the spirit is present with God).
3. **Eternal death** occurs when a person dies without accepting Christ and spends eternity separated from God.

When dealing with God's Word we must know and say the truth, the whole truth and nothing but the truth to neutralize the voice of the intruder. Therefore, it is critical to memorize Scripture. Hiding the Word in your heart will help to keep you from sinning.

VOICE OF DECEPTION: The voice of the intruder is not only the voice of doubt and denial; it is also the voice of deception. In response to Eve's inaccurate and imprecise recounting of what God said, Satan now goes in for the kill, the big lie, the deception.

> *You will **not** certainly die,"* the serpent said to the woman. *For God knows that when you eat from it your eyes will be opened, and you will be **like** God, knowing good and evil.*

30

The Contradiction: Satan has Eve exactly where he wants her. The intruder has successfully infiltrated her mind and her thinking. Firmly in his clutches, Satan is now able to contradict God's Word without any objection from her at all. *You will* <u>*not*</u> ***certainly die***. Did you notice that Satan included the word "certainly" even though Eve had left it out. *"You will* <u>*not*</u> ***certainly die***" is a lie, and not even a subtle one. It is a bold lie! It is a flagrant lie! It is an obvious lie, and yet Eve willingly accepts it. By now she may even have the fruit in her hand, examining it, and thinking, *"I touched the fruit and nothing bad happened... hmmm."* Considering Satan's lie is dangerous to do. Eve was in danger and did not even know it.

The Toxic Mixture: This is where Satan seals his deceptive deal. This is where he mixes truth with error. It's the little bit of sugar that makes the big lie easy to swallow.

> *You will* ***<u>not</u>*** *certainly die, for God knows that* ***<u>when</u>*** *you eat from it your eyes will be opened, and you will be* ***like*** *God, knowing good and evil.*

The Enticement: Satan masterfully mixes the lie with some truth. God said, *"when you* ***<u>eat</u>*** *from it you will* ***<u>certainly die</u>***.*" Satan not only contradicts the truth, but he also entices her with a partial truth. *"Your eyes will be open."* That was true. *"You will know good from evil."* That was true. It was also true that God knew the difference between good and evil, but Satan left something important out. He will usually do that. He deals in half-truths and innuendos. That's how he is able to pull you into his evil web of deception.

God only knew *about* evil simply and that was because God knows all things because He is omniscient (all-knowing). However, God did not know about evil from engaging in any evil act, therefore God remains pure and holy, separate from any and all sin. On the other hand, to eat from the tree would be an evil *act* of disobedience. They would then **know** evil by experience, which would also change their heart from the desire to only do good, to the desire to do evil.

31

The Tragedy: Even though they would know the difference between good and evil, their preference would be to do evil rather than good. That is known as the sin nature. As a result of Adam and Eve's fall, we are all born with that sin nature, the natural tendency to do evil, even though we have the knowledge of good. The Psalmist describes our plight like this. *"Surely I was sinful at birth, sinful from the time my mother conceived me"* (Psalms 51:5). The sin nature is the awful "heart disease" that we inherit from our parents. It is part of our DNA. That is bad news.

The Good News: Amid all this bad news, there is some good news. That condition we are born with does not need to be fatal. God has provided a way out, a means of escape. Through faith in Jesus Christ, you can be born again, the Holy Spirit of God will take up residence in your spirit and aid you in defeating your enemy. Why would a holy God do that? The answer is found in this well-known passage of Scripture.

> *For God so **loved** the world that he gave his one and only Son, that whoever believes in him shall not perish but have eternal life. For God did not send his Son into the world to condemn the world, but to save the world through him* (John 3:16-17, KJV).

CHAPTER 4

THE VOICES IN THE GARDEN
Satan's Success

S atan's enticement to Eve was the same prideful enticement that
got him kicked out of heaven. He wanted to be *like* God and told
Eve that eating the fruit would make her *like* God. The truth and the
tragedy are that Adam and Eve were already as close to being like
God as any created being could be. Remember, they were made in
the *"image and likeness of God."* So just like Satan, instead of
gaining more, they lost the beauty of the innocence they had in
knowing and doing only what was good. Now they knew evil and
faced difficulty doing good.

THE STRANGE VOICE
Eve gave attention to a strange voice. The voice she listened to was
not God's voice. Remember that God would come into the Garden
daily to walk and talk with Adam and Eve. He was present with them
so that they saw <u>and</u> heard him. Eve knew God's voice, that His was
the ultimate voice, and yet she obeyed a strange voice.

Eve also knew Adam's voice. He was her head and her constant
companion. But this strange voice was not the voice of her husband,
the one who had authority over her, and yet she obeyed this strange
voice. What strange voice are you listening to? Are you giving time
and attention to an unfamiliar voice?

Remember Satan often comes in disguise. Be alert! Be aware! Listen intently to God's voice and obey it. Jesus said, *"My sheep hear my voice, and I know them and they follow me"* (John 10:27). You know you belong to Jesus because you hear and strive to obey His voice and not the strange, seductive voice of Satan.

THE SILENT VOICE

In this entire episode, there is an amazingly silent voice – Adam's voice. Adam was given authority to rule over the earth and to exercise authority over the animals. Here is a strange voice, one of the animals, a snake, speaking to his wife… and Adam is… silent?

> *When the woman saw that the fruit of the tree was good for food and pleasing to the eye, and also desirable for gaining wisdom, she took some and ate it. She also gave some to **her husband, who was <u>with</u> her**, and he ate it.*

This question begs to be asked. Why is Adam silent? Why is he standing there, listening to a strange voice contradict God's voice and entice his wife and remain silent? Adam abdicated his responsibility to rule over his home (the Garden) and to assume the headship of his wife. His is the shameful, silent voice that refused to simply say what God had told him. When you hear a strange voice contradicting God's voice, do you remain silent and listen or do you counteract the strange voice with God's voice? Do you boldly declare, *"It is written!"* That is the example Jesus gave us. When He was tested by Satan in the wilderness, Jesus did have a debate or contemplate Satan's deceptive voice. He clearly and firmly declared, *"It is written"* (Matt. 4:4,7,10).

THE SEVERE VOICE

God knew the intruder was in the garden but did not intervene. Why? Because Adam was in charge! God gave him authority and would not retake that authority. Since Adam was the head, God held him responsible, not Eve. Adam blamed Eve and Eve blamed the serpent. Imagine, the ones with the rulership and the authority, blaming the animal they were given authority over. What a mess!!

Although Eve ate first, Adam was the one commanded by God; therefore, Adam had to shoulder the full responsibility for his failure to speak and guide his household the way Joshua did when he said, *"As for me and my house, we will serve the Lord"* (Joshua 24:15). A big part of the problem in our society today is that the male voice is silent, and too often it is the woman who is left to shoulder the responsibility of caring for the children and the home.

The Consequences: Now the ultimate voice speaks, and it is a severe voice, pronouncing judgment on all guilty parties:
1. the snake will crawl and eat dust all its days
2. the man would have to toil hard to earn a living
3. the woman would have pain in bearing children

But that was not the worst for the man and his wife. Oh no! They lost much more than that. Let's take a look at the totality of what they lost. They not only lost their place, but they also lost their position and they lost their power.

Loss of Place: Satan is a loser, and everyone who listens to him will also lose. As a result of Satan's rebellion, he was kicked out of heaven, no longer able to remain in the presence of God. *Like* Satan, Adam and Eve experienced the same loss. Because they heeded the Second Voice, they too lost their beautiful home and were kicked out of the Garden. If you follow Satan's voice, you will lose every time. The good news is that Christ died to restore us to our rightful place, the right to live with Him, in heaven, in His presence forever. But to have that, we must hear and heed God's voice.

Loss of Position: Instead of being more *like* God, by disobeying God's voice, they lost their exalted position, just *like* Satan. Due to his pride, Satan lost his prestigious position as an archangel in charge of leading worship. Adam and Eve lost their lofty position of God-likeness because of their willful decision to sin. Instead of being God-conscious, they became self-conscious.

Realizing they were naked, Adam and Eve tried to cover their sin with fig leaves. Instead of running to God when He came to the Garden for their daily fellowship, they hid among the trees in the Garden. What a terrible loss! Now, just *like* Satan, the first couple was no longer able to remain in the unrestricted presence of a holy, and sinless God.

Loss of Power: Adam's silence also cost them dearly. Because Adam did not use his authority to silence the Second Voice, Satan obtained a position of power as "*god*" of this world. Adam and Eve should have been ruling over this world unhindered, but by remaining silent, Adam gave place to Satan to continue to use his tactics to get us to doubt, deny and ultimately disobey God's voice. Whenever you heed the Second Voice, you can be sure that you will end up losing the place, position, and power God has destined for you to have. So the choice is yours. Whose voice will be preeminent in your life? Whose voice will you choose to obey?

The Potential: When you choose God's voice, He will restore you. But it is a choice YOU must make. IF you do, then…
1. He will **restore your place** by seating you in heavenly places with Christ (Eph. 2:6).
2. He will **restore your position** by adopting you and making you a child of the king, *a royal priesthood* (I Peter 2:9).
3. He will certainly **restore your power** by giving you the right, honor and privilege to use the authority that is inherent in the Name of Jesus.

The Power: That Name is so powerful that *at the Name of Jesus, every knee will bow and every tongue confess that Jesus Christ is Lord* (Phil. 2:10-11). There is **help** (2 Chron. 32:8), **hope** (Ps. 39:7), and **healing** (Ps. 30:2) in the Name of Jesus. Use that Name today to invite Him into your life, and then call upon the name of Jesus to help you win the battle against the tactics of the Second Voice.

CHAPTER 5

THE VOICE OF THE ACCUSER
Satan's Delight

Satan is dangerous. He has a simple, but devious strategy. He uses all of the tools at his disposal to get you to disobey God and then, when you fall, guess what he does? He approaches God and accuses you of doing wrong (Rev. 12:10). Think of it as a court scene with God as judge and Satan as the prosecutor. He brings an airtight case against you. When all of the facts are laid out, there is no doubt that you are guilty as charged. Satan takes this opportunity to taunt God, and say mocking words such as these about you:

God, You wasted your time going to all that trouble to provide salvation for _____ (insert your name). *He/she keeps messing up time and time again. In fact, I can tell that he/she does not really love You as You think. If he/she truly loved You, then they would obey You, but instead, they obey me. Actually, they often obey me without even putting up a struggle. When are You going to get wise and just give up on* _____ (insert your name)?

In order to prevent Satan from talking like that about you, it is critically important that you know and understand his strategy and prepare yourself to stand against his evil schemes (Eph. 6:11). In chapter 3, we mentioned Satan's three-prong attack to get you to doubt, deny and ultimately disobey God's voice through deception.

Now we are going to explain in detail how the Second Voice uses doubt, denial, and deception to get us to disobey God's voice.

THE MIND GAME:

Satan is a master manipulator, but most of his evil work takes place in your mind. Proverbs 23:7 inform us of this simple, but important principle. *"As a man thinks in his heart, so is he."* In other words, before you do anything, it is first a thought. Some actions like taking a shower, brushing your teeth or getting coffee on your way to work are unconscious thoughts because they have become a habit due to constant repetition. But most things that we do, we think about them ahead of time. For example:

1. What am I going to eat for breakfast?
2. I cannot work out today so I'll just do double tomorrow.
3. It cannot be morning already! I'll just hit the snooze button.
4. It's 90 degrees. What should I wear to keep cool?

When you plan your day, you might make a prioritized "to do" list to make sure you get the important things done. The list may not always work because unexpected things come up, but the point is that you think about what you are going to do *before* you do it. Well, Satan is well aware of this principle. Therefore, if he can get you to think certain thoughts, then he can get you to do the things he wants you to do. And that is precisely where Satan attacks you. The battle to get you to disobey God starts in your mind.

Strategy #1 – Doubt:

Merriam-Webster Dictionary defines doubt as:

1. to call into question the truth of
2. to lack of confidence in
3. to be uncertain

So, if Satan can get you to doubt God by calling into question the truth of God's Word, if he can get you to lack confidence in what God said, as he did with Eve, then he can get you to do exactly what he wants, which is to disobey God.

Your Weak Point: Like any good strategic fighter, your adversary the devil will attack you at your weakest point. He will look for the place where you are most vulnerable and use that area to launch his attack to get you to doubt God's Word. For example if you are single and desperate to get married because your biological clock is ticking, that becomes the target for you. So Satan says to you...

It doesn't matter that your fiancée doesn't go to church all the time. He believes in God, he just doesn't express it in the traditional way. He is such a good person, and besides, you don't have to go to church to be saved. He loves you and that's what really matters for a good marriage.

That is the Second Voice using your own desires to cast doubt in your mind, to get you to call into question the truth of God's Word, to think that God is **too strict** or **too unreasonable** especially for our modern-day living when He says:

Do not be yoked together with unbelievers. For what do righteousness and wickedness have in common? Or what fellowship can light have with darkness? What harmony is there between Christ and Satan? What does a believer have in common with an unbeliever (I Cor. 6:14-15)?

The rationale from the Second Voice is an <u>attack</u>, and you must see it as such. It is getting you to lack confidence in God's Word. God is not trying to keep something good from you. God is trying to keep you from heartache, from being united with someone who is not walking on the same path that you are. You may not see it now, or think it will be a problem later, but it's the same as saying:

God, I don't trust You with all my heart in this matter, so this time I will lean on my own limited understanding, direct my own path and go ahead and marry the "love" of my life, ignoring the fact that you only want the best for me.

Satan's strategy of doubt worked as well with you as it did with Eve. The thought now becomes an action, and Satan has won because he got you to disobey God's clear and precise Word.

It doesn't matter what example was used. Marriage to a non-believer may not be your weak point. It could be that you are already *unhappily* married, and so Satan sends the "perfect" person your way that seems to be everything your spouse is not. Remember, Satan is the deceiver. The grass only *looks* greener on the other side. Or maybe you are a foodie, you love to eat, but you are overweight, not exercising and ignoring God's Word that "*your body is the temple of the Holy Spirit*" and you must care for it.

Your Strong Link: But your weak point is not the only way Satan gets you to doubt God's Word. He will also use your strong link; the person or persons who are close to you that can influence you. He will use people that you respect as his mouthpiece of doubt just like he used Eve to influence Adam, to get him to disobey. Be careful whose advice you seek and whose advice you take. Be like Job. When his wife said to him, "*Why not curse God and die,*" Job rebuked her forcefully, refusing to do what she said (Job 2:9-10).

Strategy #2 – Deny:
Merriam-Webster Dictionary defines deny as follows:
1. to declare untrue
2. to refuse to admit or acknowledge
3. to refuse to accept the existence, truth or validity of

Satan's strategies worked so well with Eve that he continues to use them today. However, that is actually good because we can know what his evil strategies are, and we can be prepared for them. Satan got Eve to deny God's truth, and to refuse to heed God's Word when the Second Voice said, "*You will* **NOT** *certainly die*" (Gen. 3:4). She should have said what God said. Adam should have said what God said. Neither of them did. Their silence was a denial, a refusal to accept the truth and validity of what the Ultimate Voice told them. "*You must* NOT *eat from the tree of the knowledge of good and evil, for* WHEN *you eat from it you will* **certainly** *die*" (Gen. 2:17).

The Danger: In dealing with Satan's lies, silence is not golden. In fact, it is deadly! You must speak truth to Satan's lie like Jesus did when tempted in the wilderness with Satan's lies. "*It is written!*" In order to speak the truth, you must know the truth by "*hiding it in your heart*" (Ps. 119:11). Refusal to speak truth to power is to tacitly accept the lie, thereby giving power to the lie, allowing it to settle in your heart and mind. In so doing, you effectively deny the truth. And all of this happens in the battleground of the mind. We know this because Eve contemplated the enemy's words in her mind. The text tells us that Eve "**saw** *that the fruit of the tree was good for food and pleasing to the eye, and also desirable for gaining wisdom*" (Gen. 3:6). The word saw is more than just physical seeing. It also has to do with contemplating, giving thought to the lie, and disregarding the truth.

The Denial: To deny God's Word does not mean that you have to verbally contradict it. You can deny it by simply giving the lie precedence over the truth. The more you think about the lie, the more attractive it becomes, and the more attractive it becomes, the easier it is to disobey God. Be careful about giving too much thought and attention to Satan's lie. It is dangerous! It is deadly! What happened to Eve can happen to you as well. After contemplating how good and pleasing and desirable this fruit was, denying the truth that it was actually deadly, the text informs us that, "*she **took** some and **ate** it. She also **gave** some to her husband, who was with her, and he **ate** it*" (Gen. 3:6).

The Disobedience: The denial was now complete. The battle of the mind was lost. The thought that was a denial had now become an act of disobedience to God's voice. But Eve was not satisfied that she had disobeyed. She also got her husband involved in the willful act of disobedience. How *treacherous* it is to lead others into sin instead of leading them to godliness. How *appalling* it is to know God's truth, and yet be so easily influenced to disregard that truth, deny God's Word, and disobey Him. Be on guard! You are aware of the strategy of the enemy. Do not heed his voice.

Strategy #3 – Deception:

Merriam-Webster Dictionary defines doubt as follows:
1. to cause someone to accept as true what is false
2. to give a false impression

Doubt and denial lead to deception. Deception is accepting as true what is actually false. But in addition to that, Satan's deception makes you think that he will give you something that is better than what you already have, or what God has promised to give you. **What a lie!** But Eve bought it and we often do the very same thing. This was the deception that Eve bought... hook, line and did it sink her!

> *You will not certainly die. For God knows that when you eat from it your eyes will be opened, and you will be **like God**, knowing good and evil* (Gen 3:4-5).

He is the master of innuendoes that gives a false impression. Did you hear his wicked suggestion? Satan made it seem like God was holding out on them; that eating the fruit would actually be good for them, even though God said it would bring death. Satan does this to make you think that those things that God says are bad for you, are really not bad at all. His deception also makes you think that what God prohibited was actually for you and that God knew it all along, but wanted to keep you from having it.

You must understand clearly that Satan wants you to believe this... *I know the real deal. If you just listen to my voice instead of God's voice, you will be so much better off. You see, I will get you the gold at the end of the rainbow. The fame and fortune you desire will be yours. Do it my way! It is so much easier and definitely much quicker. And you will not miss out on any of the fun along the way. I promise you. God is a party pooper, but with me, you can have it all, and in half the time.*

Do not listen to his voice. Do not accept his lie. It is designed to deceive. All of it, from beginning to end is deception and like Adam and Eve, you will die if you buy into his lie.

CHAPTER 6

THE VOICE OF THE LIAR
The Father of Lies

It is certainly no surprise that the voice of the accuser is also the voice of the liar. He cannot help himself. Lies originated with Lucifer from the beginning. You do remember that the very first lie he told was the lie he said to himself. The prophet records the thoughts that were in his heart in Isaiah 14:13-14. It begins by informing us where the origin of the prideful lie took place.

*You said **in your heart**, I will ascend to the heavens; I will raise my throne above the throne of God... I will ascend above the tops of the clouds; I will make myself like the Most High.*

To be crystal clear, Jesus reiterated this fact when he confronted the Pharisees who were trying to kill Him because He told them the truth that they did not want to hear. Indeed, the truth can be painful, and the tendency is to reject it, but if you know the truth, the truth will set you free (John 8:32). So Jesus told these religious leaders, unequivocally, that they were incapable of hearing His voice because:

*You belong to your father, the devil, and you want to carry out your father's desires. He was a murderer from the beginning, not holding to the truth for there is **no truth** in him. When he lies, he speaks his native language, for he is a liar and the **father of lies** (John 8:44).*

There it is. You cannot get it any clearer than that… Satan is the Father of lies. He is the originator of lies. He is the source of lies. He can do nothing but lie. To hear his voice is to hear a lie. Do not be deceived. Why would you want to have a conversation with someone when you know that everything he says is a lie? And yet, we fall prey to the Second Voice just like Eve did in the Garden. She listened to the **big lie from the "Big I."**

> *You will not certainly die. For God knows that when you eat from it your eyes will be opened, and you will be **like God**, knowing good and evil* (Gen 3:4-5).

The Deadly Mix: Satan's lie, Satan's deception works because he cleverly mixes in partial truth with his radical lie. The outright lie is, *"You will not certainly die."* But he puts in some truth that suggests that God is holding out on them, withholding from them something that is desirable. He tells Eve, *your eyes will be **opened** and you will be more like God because you will have knowledge. You will know what God knows – **good and evil** – but He is keeping that knowledge away from you because He is not really as good to you as He pretends to be.* Of course, the exact opposite is true. Satan is the one who is pretending. He knows what the deadly results will be, but his goal is to get them to disobey God so they can suffer the loss of God's blessing, just like he did. Yes! He IS that wicked and has only evil intentions for you. Reject his voice!

The Partial Truth: The part of the mixture that was true is that their eyes would be opened and that they would know the difference between good and evil. That was all true, but it was not the whole truth. Indeed, when they ate, the text affirms, *"The eyes of both of them were opened, and they realized they were naked"* (Gen. 3:7). They now had the knowledge of good and evil. But the problem was that prior to eating, they ONLY knew good. Not knowing evil was actually good for them. But now that they knew evil as a result of their sin, Adam and Eve now realized that the knowledge of evil was detrimental, and not at all beneficial.

Adam and Eve knew evil by *experiencing* evil. Instead of only doing good, which was what God created them to know and do, now their nature was so significantly changed that their natural desire was to DO evil instead of good. True, they knew something that God knew, good and evil, but not in the same way that God knew it. You see God only knows evil because He knows ALL things. Unlike Adam and Eve, God does not know evil through experience. God is holy and without sin. The fact that He knows *about* evil, does not change or impact His holiness, but the fact that Adam and Eve knew evil through their willful disobedience has changed their nature from holiness to sinfulness. Sinning was now as natural as breathing.

The Radical Lie: But Satan's deception went even deeper than the awful mixture described above. He used his own prideful desire to deceive Eve. He wanted to be *like* God, rebelled and got kicked out of heaven. Now, he appealed to that same sense of pride when he said to Eve, if you eat the fruit, you will be *like* God. What he did not say, but what Adam and Eve should have known, was that they were already created as close to being *like* God as was possible. After all, they were already created in the ***image and likeness of God***. That meant they were created with the same character and characteristics as God – holy, loving, gracious, intelligent, faithful, kind, good, wise, etc. But they were not wise enough to reject the Second Voice. Are you wise enough to reject his deceptive voice?

The Dreadful Result: By listening to and accepting the deception of the Second Voice, instead of becoming more *like* God, they actually lost their godliness, and became more *like* Satan, more willing to listen to Satan's deceptive voice than to God's gracious voice. In fact, when God came to talk with them in the Garden, they hid from him. They should have run from Satan, instead they are hiding from God, from His very presence... but to no avail. God confronted them with their sin and punished all guilty parties: 1) the serpent had to crawl and eat dirt, 2) the man had to live by the sweat of his brow, and 3) the woman had pain in childbirth.

All these experiences were unknown prior to their prideful rebellion against God. And to top it all off, they were forced to leave their gorgeous garden home, and fend for themselves, clothe in garments of skin to cover their sin, rather than in the glorious covering of God's splendor that they were originally clothe with.

THE PLAIN TRUTH:

This is the truth, the whole truth and nothing but the truth. If you listen to the Second Voice, you will always end up losing out on the good things that God has for you. It is God who lovingly created you and has the best in mind for you... always. Even if you do not understand WHY God gives certain prohibitions or commands in His Word, even if it does not make sense to you at all, the **truth** is that God has your best interest at heart and if you obey Him you will receive the blessings He intends for you to have. You will get the opposite from the Second Voice. His promises are not true. You cannot trust him, and if you do, just like Adam and Eve, you will lose all the good things God intends for you to have.

TWO-PRONG DEFENSE: If you give Satan an inch in your life, he will take a yard. The way to deal with him is to *"**Submit** yourself to God, **resist** the devil and he will flee from you"* (Jam. 4:7). Merriam-Webster defines submit as:
  1. to yield oneself to the authority or will of another (God)
  2. to surrender, to consent to abide by the authority of (God)

Submit to God:
To submit to God is to agree to abide by the authority of His voice. That voice can be the voice of the Holy Spirit speaking to your heart or His recorded voice found in Scripture. It is a decision of your will to do what He says to do, and to refrain from doing what He prohibits. To submit *yourself* is to do so voluntarily by taking your hands off the steering wheel of your life, and placing God in the driver's seat. You willingly go in whichever direction He takes you, knowing this truth... His plan for you is to give you life more abundantly (John 10:10), a future and a hope (Jeremiah 29:11).

46

Resist the Devil:

At the same time, you are to resist the devil. Merriam-Webster, says that resist means:

1. to exert oneself so as to counteract or defeat (Satan)
2. to withstand the force or effect of (Satan)

Resisting Satan's voice requires that you exert effort and energy to counter his deceptive lies. You must work hard to resist his voice. This can only be successfully done if you know the truth of God's Word. That means you have to spend time in His Word, not only reading but studying according to 2 Timothy 2:15.

Do your best (study) *to present yourself to God as one approved, a worker who does not need to be ashamed and who correctly handles the word of truth.*

The Word of Truth is the primary weapon that you must use to resist the enemy. That's why the Word is called the *Sword of the Spirit* in Ephesians 6:17. Without the Word in your head and heart, you are defenseless against Satan's voice. But when armed with the power of the Word, spoken with a heart filled with faith, you can resist the devil, diminish his deceptive voice, and watch him flee from you. But do not let down your guard. He is a persistent enemy, always on the prowl, looking for someone to devour (1 Peter 5:8). However, if you consistently do these two things, submit yourself to God and resist the devil, you will not give Satan any opportunity to accuse you before the Father. As always, the choice is yours.

Angel of Light: Because he is the *Father* of lies, it means that Satan has children, people he can use to bring lies into your life. Paul talks about such people in 2 Corinthians 11: 13-15.

False apostles, deceitful workers, masquerade as apostles of Christ. And no wonder, for Satan himself masquerading as an angel of light. It is not surprising, then, if his servants also masquerade as servants of righteousness. Their end will be what their actions deserve.

Notice that some of the people Satan likes to use the most are those in the religious arena. They have titles that carry authority like apostles, but in reality they are deceitful workers. They use God's name, but in reality, they are deceivers, working for Satan. Pretending to speak truth, they are actually spreading Satan's lies among God's people. That is why we have to be vigilant and on the alert.

The Second Voice can and will show up in the church. But he is also fond of causing havoc in the home as well, using whoever is available to spread lies, causing confusion and division in the family. As a matter of fact, if you have ever told a lie, that was Satan using you at that moment to deceive. Understand that none of us is above being used by the enemy. If we give him a toehold, he can make it a stronghold.

So pause right now to confess any sin you may have in your life. Ask God to forgive you on the basis of His Word in I John 1:9. *"If we confess our sin, He is faithful and just to forgive us our sin and to cleanse us from all unrighteousness."* With that assurance from God, we can move forward in faith, but we must remain alert to resist the lies of the Second Voice regardless of the source – church, home, family, friends, neighbors, politicians, co-workers, etc. When someone speaks to you, be sure to look at the integrity of that person, and verify what he or she is saying against the Word of God, and what the Spirit of God is speaking to your heart. His is the Ultimate Voice that we must all listen to and obey in order to receive God's abundance.

CHAPTER 7

THE VOICE OF THE THIEF
Satan's Corrupt Character

Lucifer, the archangel, was created with magnificent beauty, externally as well as internally. But when pride rose up in his heart, and he rebelled against God's authority, his character also changed which was evidenced by a change in his name. He went from Lucifer, which means *light bearer*, to Satan which means *adversary*. Jesus described the character of our adversary, the one who opposes us, in John 10:10.

The thief comes only to steal and kill and destroy; I have come that they may have life, and have it to the full(est).

The adversary is described as a thief whose main objectives are three-fold… to *steal*, to *kill*, and to *destroy*. Let us look first at his character as a thief. Merriam-Webster describes a thief as:

1. one who unlawfully takes things that are not his or her own especially stealthily or secretly
2. one who steals with the intent to deprive the rightful owner permanently

What Satan Steals: Satan is anti-God, and desires to unlawfully steal those things that God has for us so that we can live life to the fullest. Since we get from God the *Fruit of the Spirit* – *love, joy, peace, forbearance, kindness, goodness, faithfulness, gentleness and self-control* – those are the things Satan wants to take from us.

Why Satan Steals: Satan steals from you because he is mad at God. However, he cannot get to God because God is Almighty, and infinitely more powerful than Satan. But we, you and I, are the objects of God's love.

> *For God so loved the world, He gave His one and only Son that whoever believes in Him shall not perish but have eternal life* (John 3:16, NIV).

Therefore, since Satan cannot get to God directly, he goes after Him indirectly... through us, God's children. Just like a schoolyard bully, Satan steals from you in order to hurt God. God is our Father and so when you hurt one of His children, you hurt Him as well.

Secondly, Satan steals from us because he is jealous of God's goodness in our lives. Our Father showers us with every good and perfect gift from above (James 1:17), and Satan cannot stand it. He has suffered the loss of all that he had with no hope of regaining any of it. You see, even though he caused Adam and Eve to sin, because of God's love for us, God already had in place a plan for our redemption through the death, burial, and resurrection of His Son, Jesus.

As a result, we have hope through Christ to regain what was lost through sin. Satan has no such hope! He is doomed! His fate is sealed! He will eventually end up in the Bottomless Pit for 1000 years (Rev. 20:2-3), and then thrown in the Lake of Fire for eternity (Rev. 20:10). This hopelessness causes him to rage, and so he takes it out on us by trying to steal what God has graciously given to us through His Spirit... our love, our joy, and our peace.

How Satan Steals: He uses his voice to steal from you. Yes! His voice. The Second Voice that speaks and contradicts what God says. How does he steal your love, joy and peace... by speaking fear into your heart! Fear is the opposite of faith. And fear, fear of the future, fear of the unknown will cause you to doubt, deny and disobey God. When that occurs, Satan has succeeded in his theft.

50

There is one thing that should be obvious by now. The enemy uses the same tactics over and over again. That is the reason why we do not need to be ignorant of his schemes. Since we know how he works, we can prepare ourselves and be ready against his attacks. True, he does come stealthily, and secretly, using situations and difficult circumstances in our lives:

1. to steal our faith and replace it with fear
2. to steal our peace and replace it with worry
3. to steal our love and replace it with hate
4. to steal our voice for God and replace it with silence

Take Job for example. Satan used the circumstances, the loss of all Job's wealth, the tragic loss of all ten of his children on the same day, and the loss of his health. Satan used all of this in an attempt to steal his joy, his peace and his love for the Lord, but Job did not buy into Satan's scheme. In the face of all this misfortune, this was Job's amazing response:

> *Job got up and tore his robe and shaved his head. Then he fell to the ground in worship and said: "Naked I came from my mother's womb, and naked I will depart. The Lord gave and the Lord has taken away; may the name of the Lord be praised." In all this, Job did not sin by charging God with wrongdoing.*

We can learn well from Job. Job did not deny the circumstances. Not at all! In fact, he acknowledged his grief by tearing his robe and shaving his head. These were some of the means used in Bible times and in eastern cultures to express deep grief and sorrow.

But in the midst of it all, the loss of all his wealth and in the face of 10 coffins lined up with the bodies of his 10 children, what does Job do? He fell to the ground, laying prostrate before God in an amazing act and attitude of worship. This was only possible because Job knew that God is large and in charge of his life.

Do you have that same confidence in God that Job had? So that even when the Second Voice tries to tell you that God does not love you or He would not have let this happen to you, can you maintain your love, joy, and peace, fall on your face and let your worship drown out the sound of the Second Voice? If you do that, then you will be successful in preventing the thief from stealing from you.

CHAPTER 8

THE VOICE OF THE KILLER
Satan's Corrupt Character

Whenever Satan shows up, it is for one of three reasons. We know what those three reasons are because Jesus informed us of the nature of his corrupt character when He declared:
The thief comes only to steal and kill and destroy; I have come that they may have life, and have it to the full (John 10:10).

As a thief, Satan comes to take from you what rightfully belongs to you, those blessings that were given to you by your loving Father. But his evil agenda gets worst. He not only wants to steal from you, but he also wants to *kill* you. Merriam-Webster defines kill as:
1. to deprive of life
2. to cause the death of
3. to put an end to

SATAN'S EVIL AGENDA
That sums it up. Satan is out to get you. He is not satisfied with just taking what is rightfully yours. He wants to get to you so that he can *kill* you. He wants to deprive you of life on three levels:
1. spiritually – attacks your *spirit*
2. emotionally – attacks the *mind*
3. physically – attacks the *body*

Spiritual Death: Make no mistake, Satan is your enemy and he is out to get you! He wants to kill you spiritually so he attacks your relationship with God. He wants to kill your faith in God so that you will doubt, deny and disobey him.

When you doubt God's voice, it means that you are listening to the Second Voice instead of God's voice. That places you in immediate and imminent danger of death. Why? Because doubting God's Word is just one step away from denying His Word. And if Satan can get you to do both those things, then the next most likely step is that you will disobey the voice of God.

Disobedience is sin, and sin brings separation from God. In fact, the definition of death is separation. In spiritual death, you and I are separated from the Father due to sin. That is what happened to Adam and Eve when they sinned. They died spiritually. Their God connection as they knew it was gone. Separated from God because of sin, they tried to cover their sin and shame with fig leaves (Gen. 3:7).

Finding that was not enough to cover their sin, they also hid among the trees when God came to have fellowship with them. But God could not find the man and the woman He had made in His image and likeness. So He called and asked that most piercing question, *"Adam, where are you"* (Gen. 3:9)?

Did you notice that God called Adam, not Eve? He asked Adam the question because Adam was responsible for his wife. His duty was to protect her from the evil one that had invaded their garden home. But Adam blew it. He did not use his God-given authority to resist the enemy and kick him out of his home just like God had kicked him out of heaven. Instead, he allowed his wife to listen to the Second Voice, and then willfully disobeyed the voice of God and ate the fruit. The result was instantaneous... death! They were spiritually separated from God.

Their character was now changed. Instead of being holy, they were sinful. Instead of running to God, they were hiding from Him. Instead of only knowing and doing good, they knew evil and had a difficult time doing what was good. Yes! They found out that God's Word was true. The day they ate of the fruit, sin entered and they died... spiritually separated from their sinless Creator.

The problem was that this spiritual separation from God, not only affected Adam and Eve, but all of their descendants, including you and me. We were all born with that same awful condition... spiritually separated from God. However, the condition is not final. Through faith in Christ as your Savior, through faith in Him as the One who paid the penalty for your sin, you are forgiven and that relationship with God is restored.

Nevertheless, like any relationship, it has to be maintained. The way we maintain a healthy, spiritual relationship with God is through worship, the study of His Word, listening to, and obeying His voice. Through faith, we draw close to God, and He in turn, draws close to us (James 4:8). But Satan hates that. He wants to occupy that place in your life that God occupies. Satan wants to be *like* God, so he wants you to listen to his voice instead of God's voice. That way he works to become "god" in your life and take the place and position that God alone should occupy.

The bottom line is this. If Satan can get you to doubt, deny and disobey God's voice, then you have sinned and that sin and that causes spiritual death. Do not allow Satan to kill you spiritually and negatively impact your relationship with your loving heavenly Father. So how do you stop him from gaining this victory over your life? Do what Peter instructs us to do in I Peter 5:8-9.

> *Be **alert** and of sober mind. Your enemy the devil prowls around like a roaring lion looking for someone to devour.*
> ***Resist** him, **standing firm** in the faith*

Emotional Death: Satan's goal is to kill you, the whole person. You are made up of three parts – spirit, soul (mind), and body. So he not only attacks to bring spiritual death but emotional death as well. In other words, he will attack your mind, to throw you off, and get you out of balance emotionally.

How does he do this? Easily... he does it by speaking fear into our lives about situations that we have no control over. He does it by getting you to worry about things like, 'What shall we eat?' or 'What shall we drink?' or 'What shall we wear?' instead of seeking *first* the kingdom of God and his righteousness, and then depending on your heavenly Father to take care of the needs you have (Matt. 6:31-33).

Remember, Satan's greatest battlefield is your mind. If he can get you to trust in yourself and your limited abilities instead of trusting in the Lord with all your heart (Prov. 3:5), then he will cause you to be emotionally disconnected from God. You will be unsettled, fearful and worried instead of casting all your care on the One who cares for you. Even David got downcast because of all the problems he was facing.

When David and his 600 men reached Ziklag, they found it destroyed by fire and their wives, sons and daughters taken captive. So David and his men wept aloud until they had no strength left to weep. David was greatly distressed because the men were talking of stoning him; each one was bitter in spirit because of his sons and daughters (I Sam 30:3-6).

What did David do? David found the strength to encourage himself in the Lord, to seek God's guidance, and with God's help, they were able to recapture their families. So the question is, what will you do when faced with emotional distress? Will you trust in the Lord with all your heart, as David did, and allow Him to direct your path? It is your decision. Remember, you always have a choice and the choice is always yours!

Physical Death: When God told Adam, "*the day you eat of the fruit, you will certainly die,*" both spiritual as well as physical death were the result. We know that spiritual death occurred immediately, however, because God had created Adam and Eve to live forever, it took 930 years for Adam to die physically. Of course, humans no longer live that many years. Today the average lifespan for a male in the United States is 78.6 years and for a female, it is 81.1 years. Nevertheless, physical death came into this world as a result of sin.

Satan does not have all power, but he does have power, and it seems that he has some power over physical death. When God was talking to Satan about Job and how upright he was, Satan replied that Job only served God because of the abundant blessings that he received and the hedge of protection around Job was such that Satan could not get to him to *steal, kill* or *destroy* him. So God allowed Job to be tested to show what was really in his heart. Was Satan's accusation true? Was Job's love for God genuine, or was it only because of God's goodness in Job's life? That is actually a good question for us to ask and answer. Why do you serve God? Is your love for him conditional... you love God when things are going well, but when adversity comes, do you get mad at God, turn away from God or accuse Him of not being good?

God allowed Job to be tested, but he put a limit on what Satan could do to Job. He was allowed to steal Job's possessions, he was allowed to put sickness on Job, but God restricted Satan from taking Job's life (Job 2:6). In this instance in the New Testament, there was a demon-possessed boy and the disciples could not cast out the demon, so his father brought his son to Jesus. When Jesus asked how long the boy had been in that awful state, the father explained. "*From childhood the demon has often thrown him in the fire or water to kill him*" (Mark 9:21-22). So Satan does have some power over physical death, but Jesus said, "*Do not be afraid of those who kill the body but cannot kill the soul. Rather, be afraid of the One who can destroy both soul and body in hell*" (Matt. 10:28).

The Good News: The bad news is that the goal of the thief is to steal, kill and destroy you. The good news is that he does not have all the power. Jesus does. And Jesus has given us the right and authority to use His all-powerful Name to fight the enemy when he attacks us. Will you use the powerful Name of Jesus when the Second Voice speaks to you? Do not remain silent like Adam and allow the devil to steal, kill and destroy. No! God has given you the powerful weapons of the Word, and to speak His Word in faith IN THE NAME OF JESUS. You do not need to be Satan's victim. In Christ, you are more than a conqueror. Meditate on these words in Romans 8:31-39, and use them to declare your victory!!!

> *If God is for us, who can be against us? He who did not spare his own Son, but gave him up for us all—how will he not also, along with him, graciously give us all things?*

> *Who shall separate us from the love of Christ? Shall trouble or hardship or persecution or famine or nakedness or danger or sword? No, in all these things we are more than conquerors through him who loved us.*

> *For I am convinced that neither death nor life, neither angels nor demons, neither the present nor the future, nor any powers, neither height nor depth, nor anything else in all creation, will be able to separate us from the love of God that is in Christ Jesus our Lord.*

Declare it! *Declare it!* **DECLARE IT!** In Christ you already have the victory over the enemy for greater is He that is in you than he that is in the world. But to win, you must fight! Use the weapon of the Word and the Name of Jesus. As always, the choice is yours.

CHAPTER 9

THE VOICE OF THE DESTROYER
Satan's Corrupt Character

S atan is evil and so are his intentions. That is a given. Thanks to the Word of God, and Jesus' declaration in John 10:10, we know what his evil intentions are.

The thief comes only to steal and kill and destroy; I have come that they may have life, and have it to the full.

SATAN'S EVIL AGENDA

Yes, he wants to steal the good things God has destined for you to have. Yes, Satan wants to kill you spiritually, emotionally and physically if he could. But he is not satisfied with just doing those two things. His evil intentions are such that he also wants to destroy you. Merriam-Webster defines destroy as:

1. to ruin the structure, existence or condition of
2. to put out of existence, to annihilate

The Destroyer's Targets: Satan's plan is to destroy the following:

1. Your destiny
2. Your designation (i.e. name)
3. Your purpose
4. Your foundations (i.e. home, church, institutions)

Destroy Your Destiny: God has a deep desire for everyone all of humanity. Hear God's heart in 2 Peter 3:9.

The Lord does not want anyone to perish, but everyone to come to repentance!

It does not get simpler or clearer than that. God wants everyone to be saved, to live and love Him here on earth and then spend eternity with Him as the object of His eternal love. However, the Destroyer, the enemy of God, wants the exact opposite. He wants to destroy you completely. How? By preventing you from believing the truth, which will lead to life, and getting you to believe his lie, which will destroy you. This is what the voice of The Destroyer sounds like:

This life is all there is to live for so eat, drink, and be merry. There is no such thing as hell. There is no life after death. That is all made-up baloney to stop you from having fun. So live it up. Grab all the gusto this life has to offer.

I am sure that voice is familiar. You have heard it many times from various people. Understand that The Destroyer effectively uses the voices of others to spread his destructive propaganda. This 30 second TV ad is one such willing voice, and is summarized here:

*I am an, unabashed atheist, and I'm alarmed by the intrusion by religion into our secular government. We are to keep church and state separate just as the Founding Fathers intended. Then he signed off as a "**lifelong atheist, not afraid of burning in hell.**"*

What you just read is the great lie the Destroyer wants to propagate because it keeps people separated from God here on earth, and anyone who dies physically without accepting Christ will end up spending eternity with Satan in hell (i.e. the Lake of Fire).

*And the devil who **deceived** them was thrown into the lake of fire and will be tormented day and night forever… Anyone whose name was not found written in the book of life was thrown into the lake of fire (Rev. 20:10, 15).*

The Second Voice is the voice of the Destroyer, and if you listen to that voice, you will be destroyed along with him. How ironic it is that the ultimate destiny and destination for the Destroyer is *destruction*. Satan hates you so much, he wants to deceive you so that your destiny can be the same as his – total destruction. The only question that remains is... will you listen to the voice of the Destroyer or to the voice of the One who came *that you might have life to the fullest* (John 10:10). The choice is yours!

Destroy Your Designation: If you are a believer, your name, your designation, is Christian. In other words, you bear the name of Christ, and whatever you do, will reflect on His Name. So if the Destroyer can get you to doubt, deny and disobey God's Word, if he can get you to fall into gross sin, then he can destroy your good name. This then affects your witness, and your reputation, which can negatively impact your usefulness to God.

Destroy Your Purpose: The Voice of the Destroyer is such that it works to destroy you internally and externally. When your reputation is destroyed; that is external and it is visible for all to see. However, the Destroyer also speaks lies *to* you, *about* you in order to destroy your purpose. He will say things like this about you:

Who do you think you are anyway? What makes you think you can accomplish that? God is unreasonable to even ask you to do that. Why bother? If you try and fail, everyone will laugh at you. It's best for you to play it safe and just do what you have always done.

The evil Voice of the Destroyer is so familiar. He may speak directly to you words that spawn self-doubt and lack of faith in the God who called you to step out on faith. Or the Destroyer may use those close to you to speak words of discouragement with the intent to destroy your purpose. If he can plant seeds of doubt in your mind and prevent you from fulfilling the purpose God has for you, then Satan has won the victory. Since you know what his evil agenda is, do not succumb to it. Fulfill your purpose!

Destroy the Foundations: Satan is never satisfied. He is always on the prowl looking for someone or something to destroy. And so, true to form, in addition to individuals, Satan also focuses his attacks on the foundations that make us strong as a people and as a nation. Those foundations are institutions such as the family, marriage, the church, and government. That is the reason the Psalmist asks this question that we are compelled to answer:

When the foundations are being destroyed, ***what can the righteous do*** *(Ps. 11:3)?*

There has been an on-going attack on the family and on marriage. In fact, the nuclear family composed of husband, wife and children is no longer the norm. The divorce rate in the United States is 50%.

Marriage and the Family: For subsequent marriages, the divorce rate is even higher. In fact, the length of the average marriage is only 8.2 years. The family is the foundation of the society and so Satan can do a lot of damage by destroying marriages either through a divorce or through people simply living together without the benefit of marriage. So what can the righteous do? We can work to strengthen marriages through marriage ministries in churches, conferences, seminars, counseling, etc. Through these means, we can help husbands to learn to listen to God's voice and to love their wives as Christ loved the church (Eph. 5:25). Wives can learn the wisdom of submitting to their husbands as to the Lord (Eph. 5:22). These are God's instructions in Titus 2:2-8 that teach us how to keep the foundations strong. This enables husbands and wives to bear the Name of Christ without smearing His Name by our behavior.

For Older Men and Women: *Teach the older men to be temperate, worthy of respect, self-controlled, sound in faith, in love and in endurance. Teach the older women to be reverent in the way they live, not to be slanderers or addicted to much wine, but to teach what is good.*

For Young Women: *The older women can urge the younger women to love their husbands and children, to be self-controlled and pure, to be busy at home, to be kind, and to be subject to their husbands, so that no one will malign the word of God.*

For Young Men: *Similarly, encourage the young men to be self-controlled. In everything set them an example by doing what is good. In your teaching show integrity, seriousness and soundness of speech that cannot be condemned, so that those who oppose you may be ashamed because they have nothing bad to say about us.*

That is God's voice instructing His people, the church as well as the pastor on how to keep the family and the home strong in order to withstand the attacks of the Destroyer.

The Church: The problem is this. Satan also attacks the church. The very vehicle that God uses to keep the home strong is also under attack, and the church is therefore declining. Between 6,000 and 10,000 churches in the United States die every year, which means that around 100 to 200 churches will close their doors this week (Shull, 2018). Nearly 50% of Americans have no church home, and half of all U.S. churches did not add any new members to their ranks in the last two years (Krejoir, 2007). Over 1,500 pastors leave the ministry every month, and about 3,500 people a day leave the church. Given those statistics, it may not come as a surprise that the profession of "Pastor" is near the bottom of a survey of the most respected professions, just above that of "car salesman" (Statistics, 2018).

When the foundations are being destroyed, **what can the righteous do** – PRAY! We have to pray because we know that the gates of hell cannot prevail against the church (Matt. 16:18), but that does not stop Satan from attacking the church, its pastors and its leaders.

The diminishing influence of the church in the society diminishes the prevalence of God's voice and it amplifies the Second Voice. We cannot afford to let the Destroyer win the battle within the culture that says the church is hypocritical and no longer relevant for dealing with the complex issues facing our society today.

The Government: God has established governmental authority to keep order in the society. In the Old Testament, God ruled over Israel in a theocracy, with the 613 commandments of the Mosaic Law as their Constitution (Dennery, 2009). Today, we live under a democracy that is also built around a Constitution, a system of laws to govern the people, to keep order and to punish wrongdoers. According to Romans 13:1-5, this is God's foundational purpose for government.

> *Let everyone be subject to the governing authorities, for there is no authority except that which God has established. The authorities that exist have been established by God. Whoever rebels against the authority is rebelling against what God instituted and will bring judgment on themselves. For rulers hold no terror for those who do right, but for those who do wrong. Do you want to be free from fear of the one in authority? Then do what is right and you will be commended. For the one in authority is God's servant for your good. But if you do wrong, be afraid, for rulers do not bear the sword for no reason. They are God's servants, agents of wrath to bring punishment on the wrongdoer. Therefore, it is necessary to submit to the authorities, not only because of possible punishment but also as a matter of conscience.*

Governmental authority is supposed to keep citizens safe and to punish the wrongdoer. But when that authority becomes corrupt so that it slaps the wrist of the powerful and rich child rapist while sending the poor person who commits a relatively minor offense to jail for 20 years with the pretense of being "tough on crime," then the foundation is being destroyed. According to Proverbs 29:2…

*When the righteous are in authority, the people rejoice;
when the wicked rule, the people groan.*

The Destroyer attacks the foundations, the institutions that God put in place for the benefit of the people. He postures himself against what Christ did so that we can have life and have it more abundantly (John 10:10). So we have to stand firm as individuals against his attacks, and pray fervently for the institutions that are needed for us to thrive as God's intended. As God's people, it is our responsibility to pray because the prayer of the righteous is powerful and effective (James 5:16). The choice is yours. What will you do?

PART TWO
THE PRESCRIPTION

THE VOICE OF THE SHEPHERD

THE EAR OF THE HEARER

THE POWER OF THE BELIEVER

THE PRACTICE OF THE DISCIPLE

THE ARMOR OF THE WARRIOR

OVERVIEW OF PART TWO
THE PRESCRIPTION

In part one of this book, we reviewed the various strategies of Satan and his evil efforts to steal, kill and destroy. In part two, we are taking an in-depth look at the prescription, the strategies that are available to us in order to fight and defeat the deception of the Second Voice. First and foremost is the strategy to listen to the voice of the Shepherd who speaks the truth. But in order to do so, you must have an ear to hear and obey the Shepherd's voice. When you do this, that places you in a position to use the power that is available to you. This is the power that is found in the Name that is above every name – Jesus. If you follow Christ as a true disciple and put on the full armor of God daily, then you will be able to stand against the schemes of the enemy. The battle that you are in is indeed winnable, even though the enemy is formidable. However, you must be steadfast in using all the tools that are available to you.

CHAPTER 10

THE VOICE OF THE SHEPHERD

Did you notice that in describing the character of Satan, Jesus also makes a contrast between His own character and that of Satan? Satan's self-initiated agenda is to steal, to kill and to destroy. That is who he is and what he does.

Jesus' agenda is the exact opposite. He came so that we could live life to the fullest (John 10:10). Christ's agenda is based on the nature of His self-described character that is rooted and grounded in love (I Jn. 4:8). Jesus said this about Himself in John 10:11-13.

> *I am the Good Shepherd. The good shepherd lays down his life for the sheep. The hired hand is not the shepherd and does not own the sheep. So when he sees the wolf coming, he abandons the sheep and runs away. Then the wolf attacks the flock and scatters it. The man runs away because he is a hired hand and cares nothing for the sheep.*

The contrast could not be more stark! The analogy could not be more fitting! Jesus is the Good Shepherd. Satan is the wolf. You and I are the sheep. When the wolf comes to steal, kill and destroy His sheep, the Good Shepherd is the One who protects and defends the sheep to the extent that He literally lays down His life for the His sheep. Why? We belong to Him. He claims us as His own. The hired hand will run away from the attacker, but not the shepherd.

THE SHEPHERD'S VOICE IS:

The Voice of Power: When the Shepherd speaks, He speaks with power and with absolute authority. The Psalmist explains the magnitude of the power of His voice when he declared:
> *He spoke, and it came to be; he commanded, and it stood firm* (Psalms 33:9).

In other words, God spoke the worlds into existence by the mere power of His spoken word... *Let there be*. And yet with all that power and authority, He gives humans a free will. We can choose to accept Him or reject Him, to obey His voice or to do as we please. Ironically, all the rest of creation obeys Him without question. On His command...

1. the waters of the Red Sea parted (Exodus 14:21)
2. the big fish swallowed Jonah and did not eat him for 3 days and 3 nights (Jonah 1:17)
3. the sun stood still for 24 hours, giving Joshua complete victory over the Amorites (Joshua 10:13)
4. the mega storm on the Sea of Galilee became calm instantaneously when He spoke and said, *"Peace, be still"* (Mark 4:39).

Indeed, humans are the only ones who question the Voice of the Shepherd and have the audacity to debate whether to obey His voice or not. What makes Him so amazing is that although He has the power, The Shepherd does not force anyone to obey His voice. Rather, His desire is that we choose to listen to His voice. Our obedience is a test of our love for Him. *If you love Me, keep my commandments* (John 14:15).

The Voice of Truth: The Shepherd speaks the truth, the whole truth and nothing but the truth. In fact, He IS truth! That is why He can say without fear of contradiction:
> *If you hold to my **teaching**, you are really my disciples. Then you will know the truth, and the truth will set you free* (John 8:31-32).

70

That is so very clear. The Shepherd's voice instructs the sheep and makes the truth of God's Word clear, easy to understand, and to follow. When you listen to the Shepherd's voice you can be *certain* that you will hear the truth. But if you listen to the Second Voice, you can be just as *certain* that you will hear lies.

The Voice of Faith: When the Shepherd speaks, He does so in order to empower you with faith. You see, *faith comes by hearing the Word of God* (Rom. 10:17). Therefore, anyone who desires or needs faith, the only requirement is that you listen to His voice. The more you listen, the more your faith grows just like the tiny mustard seed grows to produce the biggest bush. Do you want more faith? If so, then increase the quantity and the quality of the time you spend listening to the Voice of the Shepherd.

The Voice of Love: The Shepherd loves His sheep. Therefore, when He speaks to them, He speaks with a heart and a voice of love. His love is unmistakable and His love undeniable. Romans 5:6-8 explains the depth of His love for us:

> *You see, at just the right time, when we were still powerless, Christ died for the ungodly. 7 Very rarely will anyone die for a righteous person, though for a good person someone might possibly dare to die. 8 But God demonstrates his own love for us in this: While we were still sinners, Christ died for us.*

You see, the Shepherd does not only say that you are His *beloved*; He also calls you the *"apple of His eye"* (Ps. 17:8). He loves you supremely because He gave you the greatest gift possible – His life. He willingly laid down His life, died, and rose from the dead so you can have abundant life here and now, and eternal life forever in His presence. That is love! So when you hear His voice, He whispers sweet *"somethings"* in your ear such as: *I love you with an everlasting love* (Jeremiah 31:3), *you are fearfully and wonderfully made* (Psalms 139:14), *ask anything according to My will and you will have it* (I John 5:14-15).

71

So, how should you respond to the love of the Shepherd? Simple! By returning His love. He is the *Supreme Lover*; therefore. you cannot find love anywhere that will match His. When you receive and return His love, your heart will finally, truly be satisfied, overflowing with the greatest love from the greatest lover.

The Voice of Wisdom: *He founded the world by His wisdom and stretched out the heavens by His understanding* (Jer. 10:12), so the all-wise Shepherd urgently begs you to heed His words of wisdom that He has prescribed for your success:
> *Keep this Book of the Law always on your lips; meditate on it day and night, be careful to do everything written in it. Then you will be prosperous and successful* (Joshua 1:8).

The Voice of Forgiveness: The voice of the Shepherd is a tender voice; a voice that is always ready to forgive. He did so for the woman caught in the very act of adultery. Brought to Jesus by the religious leaders to condemn her, He made a simple, but piercing declaration. *"Let anyone of you who is without sin be the first to throw a stone at her"* (John 8:7).

Because none fit the criteria of sinlessness other than Jesus Himself, He was the only One who qualified to condemn her. Instead, He forgave her and gave her this command. *Neither do I condemn you. Go and leave your life of sin* (John 8:11). And the Good Shepherd has the same words of forgiveness for you that He had for the woman. This is His directive to us in I John 1:9.
> *If we confess our sin, He is faithful and just and will forgive our sin and cleanse us from all unrighteousness.*

But He does not stop there. Since you are forgiven, He expects you to extend the same grace to others and forgive those who have wronged you. Knowing the grace, which has been extended to you that you did not earn and do not deserve, you and I should be more than willing to extend that same grace of forgiveness to our family and friends, and our brothers and sisters in Christ.

72

The Voice of Hope: The Shepherd's voice is a voice of hope. To hope, according to Merriam-Webster is to desire with expectation of fulfillment. That is the essence of what the Shepherd provides for the sheep. He says these words of hope directly to you:

I know the plans I have for you. Plans to prosper you and not to harm you. Plans to give you hope and a future (Jeremiah 29:11).

Because He has showered His love upon you, because He has forgiven you and given to you eternal life, because He has the best plan already laid out for your life; this is the blessed hope that you can look forward to and it comes straight from the heart of the Shepherd to your heart.

I go and prepare a place for you so I will come again, and receive you unto myself; that where I am, there ye may be also... and will present you faultless, before the presence of My glory with exceeding great joy (John 14:3, Jude 1:24 KJV).

Your Response to His Voice: The only question that remains is this, how will you respond to the Voice of the Shepherd? This should be a no-brainer. The Shepherd has given so much *for* you – His very life. He has given so much *to* you – truth, faith, love, wisdom, forgiveness, hope, and the list goes on. The only appropriate response is to hear and to heed the Voice of the Shepherd. Obey His voice willingly. Submit to Him so that you can receive ALL that He has planned, purposed and destined for your life. You will indeed be better off as result. As you journey through this life with all its challenges, you can rest assured that the Good Shepherd will be with you every step of the way, and His voice will be there to guide and lead you so that you arrive at the final destination – the heavenly home He has lovingly prepared for you to occupy, in His presence for all eternity.

CHAPTER 11

THE EAR OF THE HEARER

The Voice of the Shepherd is not only a good voice, but it is also the exact opposite of the Second Voice whose agenda is to steal, kill and destroy. This is the declaration the Good Shepherd makes to His sheep. *I have come that you may have life and have it to the fullest* (John 10:10), rich abundant life here and now. But there is a prerequisite to qualify for that promise of abundant life.

*My sheep **listen** to my voice; I **know** them, and they **follow** me. I **give** them eternal life, and they shall never perish; no one will snatch them out of my hand. My Father, who has given them to me, is greater than all; no one can snatch them out of my Father's hand* (John 10:27-29).

The qualification for the sheep is simple, "***My*** *sheep* <u>*listen*</u> *to my* ***voice***." If you belong to the Shepherd, then you will listen to His voice. Merriam-Webster defines listen as:

1. to hear something with thoughtful attention
2. to be alert to catch an expected sound

How does the shepherd guide His sheep? By speaking! Therefore, the sheep must listen to the voice of the shepherd. Listening is not an option; it is an imperative! To listen is to do more than just hear the words spoken; it is to do more than just give thoughtful attention. To listen is to hear AND obey the Shepherd's voice.

How To Amplify The Shepherd's Voice

It is imperative to listen to the Shepherd in order to drown out the noise of Second Voice. Remember that Satan, the adversary goes about like a roaring lion, seeking whom he can destroy. That means that Satan's voice is loud and boisterous, making it easier to hear his voice than the voice of the Shepherd. Although it is not possible to completely silence the roar of the adversary, it is possible to diminish Satan's voice and to amplify the Shepherd's voice. The remainder of this chapter explains **how** to listen so that you can hear loudly and clearly the still, small Voice of the Shepherd.

Listen Willingly: To hear the Shepherd's voice, you must first have an *ear to hear*. In other words, listening starts with an open mind and heart, a desire to hear and receive the truth. You must be one of His sheep to have a *"hearing ear."* That is the reason Jesus often ended His teaching by saying, *whoever has ears to hear, let him hear* (Mt. 11:15, 13:9,43; Mark 4:9,23, 7:16; Luke 8:8, 14:35). Jesus knew that some followed Him, not to listen to His teaching, but for the food (i.e. fish and loaves) they could get from Him (John 6:26). What is your desire? Is it to hear the truth? Then **you** must open **your** ears to hear what the Shepherd is saying to you. It is an act of your will. Do not let this be Jesus' indictment of you.

> *Because I tell the truth, you do not believe me! If I am telling the truth, why don't you believe me? Whoever belongs to God hears what God says. The reason you do not hear is that you do not belong to God* (John 8:45-47).

Listen Intentionally: An *ear to hear* also means that you listen intentionally by making it a priority to set aside time to listen to His voice. This is quality time, not when you are exhausted, but when you have taken time to be still, to shut out the noise of the day and to intentionally focus so that you can hear that still, small voice as He speaks. The quality and quantity of time you set aside intentionally will reveal how serious you really are about listening so that you can hear His voice.

Listen Internally: To really listen, you must not only hear with your ears, but with your heart as well. God is Spirit, and so our communication with Him must also be Spirit to spirit. Often that still, small voice that we hear is Holy Spirit communicating with our spirit. That's why you must be born again, born of the Spirit in order to hear Him when He speaks.

Listen Patiently/Passionately: Listening often requires patience. Why? We do not always get an *immediate* answer to what we are seeking God for. While you are patiently waiting for the answer, there should be some passionate expectation of getting the answer. Your passion surrounds the anticipation, not only of what He will say but also what He will do in and through your life as a result.

Listen Prayerfully: *Can you hear Me now*? This is a frequent mantra when we are on our cell phones and we hit a dead zone or we are in a building that blocks the signal. The same thing can happen when Jesus is speaking. We may not be able to hear Him because we are in a dead zone called "sin" that interrupts the signal. There may be a blockage that puts us on a different frequency so that we are unable to hear. That's why prayer is so vital for hearing the Voice of the Shepherd. Prayer gives us access to God in the Name of Jesus. Through prayer, we can repent, ask for forgiveness, and be back in tune with the Spirit so we can clearly hear His voice.

Listen Consistently: Listening to the Shepherd's voice needs to be a consistent habit, not a haphazard, once-in-awhile event. To listen is to spend time getting to know the Shepherd and His voice. but consistently, continually so that it becomes the norm. Because you are developing a relationship with the Shepherd, make this time a special time, a date with the Shepherd, so that your "*us time*" is time together that you do not break. Position yourself to hear Him speak to you by reading His Word, and spending time in His presence, and in worship as you dwell in the secret place of the Most High. You will find Him waiting for you for your special *time*.

76

Listen Obediently: Engaging in the above – listening willingly, intentionally, internally, patiently, passionately, prayerfully, and consistently – will be futile unless you purpose in your heart to obey what you hear. That is the bottom-line, obedience to the voice of the Shepherd. Jesus said it this way:

Why do you call me, 'Lord, Lord,' and do not do what I say (Luke 6:46)?

After all, the blessing is in obeying the Word that He has spoken to you. Obedience results in your good and His glory. Proverbs, the book of wisdom explains the benefits that accrue as a result of being doers of the Word and not hearers only (James 1:22).

*Pay attention to what I say; turn your ear to my words. Do not let them out of your sight; keep them within your heart; for **they are life** to those who find them **and health** to one's whole body* (Proverbs 4:20-22).

One Final Question: If the roaring lion Satan is making so much noise, why doesn't Jesus, the ***Conquering Lion of the Tribe of Judah*** make more noise, and make His voice louder than Satan's? The answer is simple. The Shepherd will not compete with Satan for your attention. He wants you to seek Him because His ultimate desire is to have a relationship with you. That in-depth relationship requires time in order to get to know one another. Knowing the voice of a loved one comes from spending time with that person. And that's what Jesus desires above all else. Time spent with Him indicates your desire to be with Him, to know Him and to be able to hear His still, small voice even in the midst of a lot of noise. A shouting match with Satan would simply be too noisy, and way too confusing, making it difficult to distinguish the true voice of the Shepherd. To hear His still, small voice means you have to get **up close and personal** so that you can distinguish His voice from every other voice that seeks your attention. And then, knowing His voice, and hearing His voice, will you obey His voice? The choice is yours. The choice is *always* yours! What will you do?

CHAPTER 12

THE POWER OF THE BELIEVER

Indeed, the believer has power over the enemy based on Jesus' words in Luke 10:19a. *I have given you authority over all the power of the enemy* (NLT). But let's be very clear. This power is not inherent power that we have; rather it is delegated power. Merriam-Webster defines delegate as:

1. to entrust to another
2. to assign responsibility or authority
3. to appoint as one's representative

THE PURPOSE OF THE POWER

To Build His Church: Therefore, the power we have is actually God's power that He has entrusted to us. Because the use of His power is a sacred trust, He has <u>assigned</u> us with the task to *build His church* so that it can withstand the attacks of the enemy.

*On this rock I will build my church, and the gates of Hades (hell) will not overcome it. I will **give** you the keys of the kingdom of heaven; whatever you bind on earth will be bound in heaven, and whatever you loose on earth will be loosed in heaven* (Matthew 16:18-19).

To Be His Ambassadors: He has <u>appointed</u> us as His ambassadors with the authority to represent Him here on earth as we build His church by preaching the gospel to everyone (Mark 16:15).

He has committed to us the message of reconciliation. We are therefore Christ's ambassadors, as though God were making his appeal through us. We implore you on Christ's behalf: Be reconciled to God.

THE SOURCE OF THE POWER
The power that God has delegated to us comes from three primary sources:
1. The Power of His Name
2. The Power of His Word
3. The Power of the Holy Spirit

The Unlimited Power of Jesus: After Jesus rose from the dead and before He returned to the Father, He made this definitive statement about His power. *All power in heaven and on earth has been given to me* (Matthew 28:19). Jesus has unlimited power and has delegated that unlimited power to us to use to build His church, as well as to be His ambassadors to the lost.

THE POWER OF HIS NAME:
His Supreme Name: His unlimited power is demonstrated by the fact that His Name is so powerful that it is exalted above every other name. Philippians 2:9-11 says it like this:
*God exalted him to the highest place and gave him **the Name** that is above every name, that at the name of Jesus every knee should bow, in heaven and on earth and under the earth, and every tongue acknowledge that Jesus Christ is Lord, to the glory of God the Father.*

Our Supreme Right: There is no name that is greater than the Name of Jesus. For those who have accepted His supreme sacrifice on the cross for our sin, we have been adopted into the family of God. As believers, as members of God's family, we have certain rights and privileges. One of those rights is the authority to use the powerful Name of Jesus.

Pray In His Name: Jesus has given us access to the very throne room of Heaven, to the power of the Triune God – Father, Son, and Holy Spirit – by giving us the authority to use His Name when we pray. Since He has access to the Father, He gives us the authority to make requests of the Father through the power of His Name.

You did not choose me, but I chose you and appointed you so that you might go and bear fruit—fruit that will last—and so that whatever you ask in my name the Father will give you.

This is the reason that we address our prayer to the Father and we end our prayer with "*in the Name of Jesus.*" That is the authority that Jesus gave us – the right to pray and to make requests of the Father in His Name.

This is the confidence we have in approaching God: that if we ask anything according to his will, he hears us. And if we know that he hears us—whatever we ask—we know that we have what we asked of him (I John 5:14-15).

Indeed, we can have confidence in our prayers and know its not just speaking words. His guarantee is that anything we ask that is based on His will, we will have. We know what His will is because His will is revealed in His Word.

Paul's Example: We have an excellent example of the use of delegated power by the early church in the book of Acts. Peter and John went to the Temple to pray and encountered a man who was lame from birth, sitting at the gate called Beautiful, begging for money. Using his right to ask

Silver or gold I do not have, but what I do have I give you. **In the name of Jesus Christ** *of Nazareth,* **WALK***. Taking him by the right hand, he helped him up, and instantly the man's feet and ankles became strong. He jumped to his feet and began to walk. Then he went with them into the temple courts, walking and jumping, and praising God* (Acts 3:6-8).

The power that the believer has is the power to use the powerful Name of Jesus. We can use that Name at any time. Obviously, we can use it during the times of formal prayer, individual prayer or corporate prayer. And we can use the Name of Jesus against the attacks of the enemy. When the Second Voice tries to speak to you or get you to do something wrong, you can command him "*In the Name of Jesus*" to be silent or to leave.

Jesus' Example: That is exactly what Jesus did when Satan tested him for forty days and nights in the wilderness. It was the third time when Satan wanted Him to bow down and worship him (Matt. 4:8-9). Jesus spoke to Satan and literally told him to go away:

> *Jesus said to him, "Away from me, Satan! For it is written: 'Worship the Lord your God, and serve him only. Then the* ***devil left him***, *and angels came and attended him* (Matt. 4:10-11).

It's Your Power; Use It! Yes, Jesus told Satan to leave and he did. With the power and authority you have from Jesus, you can do the same thing. You do not need to listen to Satan's deceptive voice. You see, that is the same authority Adam had in the Garden, to command the serpent to leave because God had given him dominion over the animals. But, to his detriment, he remained silent. You cannot afford to remain silent. You have been given power and authority, but it is not automatic. You have to USE IT in order to obtain the benefit. By using the authority of Jesus' Name, you can command Satan to go "*away from me.*"

THE POWER OF HIS WORD:
In addition to using the Name of Jesus to fight against the attack of the enemy, the power of the believer is in using the Word of God.

> *The word of God is alive, and powerful, and sharper than any double-edged sword* (Heb. 4:12).

The Word is the believer's offensive and defensive weapon that is why it is a double-edged sword.

81

Our Defensive Weapon: By now we are well aware of the tactics of the enemy. The Second Voice attacks believers in their minds, with words designed to deceive. His purpose is to get us to doubt, deny, and then disobey God's Word. But we have a powerful weapon against Satan's attack. It is the Word of God spoken by the believer. The Word, spoken aloud to correct the lies of the Second Voice, is the same defense that Jesus used against Satan's attack. He declared, "*It is written*" (Matt. 4).

Jesus fought and won with the Word and so will you. That is why it is so critically important for you to "*study to show yourself approved by God*" (2 Tim. 2:15), so that you will not be deceived. Remember, his lies are subtle and often mixed with a measure of truth, so it is crucial that you *know* the truth. It is the truth of God's Word, spoken by you, that will defeat the voice of the destroyer. When you declare the truth of God's Word, it will not only *set* you free (John 8:32), it will *keep* you free.

Our Offensive Weapon: The Sword of the Word is a double-edged because it is not only a defensive weapon; it is also an offensive weapon. The psalmist explains it this way.

How can a young person stay on the path of purity? By living according to your Word... I have hidden your word in my heart that I might not sin against you (Ps. 119:9, 11).

The psalmist asks and answers the pertinent question. The way in which a person, young or old, can stay pure is by living according to God's Word. The psalmist informs us that the way to live holy is by hiding the Word in your heart. Joshua comes to the rescue to explain exactly HOW to hide the Word in our hearts.

*Keep this Book of the Law always **on your lips; meditate on it** day and night, so that you may be careful to do everything written in it. Then you will be prosperous and successful* (Joshua 1:8).

The Book of the Law refers to the first five books of the Bible because that is all that was written at the time. Today, we have the entirety of God's Word, all sixty-six books. So God gives Joshua the three-step process for hiding the Word in your heart to build up your spirit so that you can increase the volume of God's voice, and at the same time minimize the volume of the Second Voice.

STEP 1 – Read the Word: The first step for hiding the Word in your heart is to read the Word, preferably aloud (Psalms 119:11-13). Why? Simple. Romans 10:17 tells us, *"faith comes by **hearing** the Word."* If you want to develop faith to believe God's Word, you must **hear** it. Yes, you can read the Word silently, but to get the maximum effect, you need to read the Word aloud.

Another option available is to use technology to hear the Word. You can use any of the many available Bible websites and apps to find the passage you want and click the audio icon. It will read the passage for you so that you can **hear** the Word. As you listen, your faith will grow so that you will walk (live) by faith, not by sight (2 Cor. 5:7). How often do you read the Word... aloud?

STEP 2 – Meditate on the Word: According to Merriam-Webster to meditate is:
1. to **focus** one's thoughts on (i.e. the Word)
2. to **reflect** on or ponder over (i.e. the Word)

To meditate on God's Word is to focus your thinking on His Word, to think deeply, not only about what it says but what it means. The idea of meditating also involves memorizing the Word so that it is always with you, and available to use to combat the Second Voice on the spot. That is what Jesus did. He had the Word in His heart and could quote it on the spot. He did not need to go and find the scroll to look up the text. Because it was in His heart, He could speak it, minimize the Second Voice and win the victory over temptation. Do you follow Jesus' example by meditating and memorizing the Word to avoid succumbing to the voice of the enemy?

STEP 3 – Do the Word: If you consistently do steps 1 and 2 on a daily basis, then step 3 should follow. You see, Proverbs 23:7 says, "*as a man* (person) *thinks in his heart, so is he*" (KJV). In other words, your thoughts become your actions. What you think about and reflect on regularly is what you will do. So, if you are reading and studying God's Word, if you are meditating and memorizing God's Word regularly and consistently, then you will do the Word and not sin against God. The Word that is deep down in your heart and at the same time readily available on your lips, is sufficient to guard your heart against the voice of the enemy so that you stay prepared, ready to fight and ready to win!

THE POWER OF THE HOLY SPIRIT:

The third source of power the believer has to fight the attacks of the enemy is the Holy Spirit. The Holy Spirit is the third person of the Trinity, which is comprised of the Father, Son, and Holy Spirit. One of the functions of the Holy Spirit is to empower the believer to do what is right. The text, Philippians 2:13, explains it this way.

> *For it is God* (the Holy Spirit) *who works **in** you to will* and *to act in order to fulfill His good purpose.*

Internal Power: What's so great about the Holy Spirit is that He works from the inside out. Your body is the temple of the Holy Spirit (1 Cor. 6:19), therefore He resides in you and with you 24/7 to give you the power to live a holy life. He does this in two primary ways. First, He gives you the will, the *desire* to do what is right by reminding you of the Word that you have read or heard. Second, He encourages you to act, to live in concert with that Word so that you can have the abundant life and fulfill the plan God has destined for your life. The only question is, *"Will you appropriate the power of the Spirit?"* You see, it is up to you to plug into your power source just like you plug in your cell phone to charge it. Holy Spirit's power is always there, but when He speaks to you and encourages you on the right path, it is up to you to *"plugin"* to the power of His voice and obey. The choice is yours. The choice is *always* yours. What will you do?

84

CHAPTER 13

THE PRACTICE OF THE DISCIPLE

A disciple is a learner, a follower of Christ. Jesus made this clear in the Great Commission found in Matthew 28:19-20 where He commanded His disciples to:

> Go, and **make disciples** of all nations, baptizing them... and **teaching them** to obey everything I have commanded you.

Making Disciples: Jesus' command lets us know that making disciples is essential. When Jesus was here on earth, one of the first things He did was to select twelve special disciples. But make no mistake; Jesus had many more disciples than the twelve that were His core group. There were thousands who followed Him. And what did Jesus do? He diligently **taught** them. What is commonly referred to as the "*Sermon on the Mount*" (Matthew 5 to 7) was *not* preaching, but Jesus actually teaching His as stated in Matthew 5:2 which says, "*Jesus began to **teach** them.*" So, as Jesus is getting ready to return to the Father, He commissions His disciples to go and make more disciples by *teaching* them to obey what Jesus had already taught them.

The Fundamentals: Since learning is so important to the making of a disciple, the question that begs to be asked is, "*What are the fundamentals a believer needs to learn in order to be a disciple, and how do they help us to defeat the enemy?*"

The 5 Fundamentals of Discipleship: There are five fundamental areas of knowledge that are critical for making disciples. They are 1) *prayer* 2) *worship*, 3) *study of the Word*, 4) *stewardship* and 5) *evangelism* (Dunnigan & Dennery, 2018, p. 26). When a believer not only learns but practices these fundamentals of discipleship, then he or she is able to fight and win when attacked by the enemy.

1) THE FUNDAMENTAL OF PRAYER:

Prayer is ***talking*** to God **and** *listening* to His voice. Time spent with God in prayer, on a daily basis, helps to develop an intimate relationship with Him. In addition, prayer is also a personal declaration of dependence on God. It is an admission that you need Him, you need His help to live holy, and that your hope, trust, and confidence is in Him *alone* (Dunnigan & Dennery, 2018).

The Practice of Prayer: The best way to learn to pray is by praying; talking to God as a friend would talk with their friend. There is a place for teaching a disciple how to pray. Even His 12 disciples asked Jesus, "*Lord, teach us to pray.*" But there is no substitute for the daily practice of prayer to amplify the voice of God and to diminish the voice of the enemy. What is your prayer life like? Is it vibrant and exciting or is it dull and barely existent? Only you can answer that question and make the appropriate changes as needed.

2) THE FUNDAMENTAL OF WORSHIP:

The purpose of worship is to glorify, honor, praise, exalt, and please God. You were created to worship God, not because God needed anyone, but because He desired to have an intimate relationship with you. During worship you are able to enter into God's presence, and pour out your love on Him while basking in the warmth of His great love for you because you are the apple of His eye. As a result of the New Covenant, established through Jesus' death and resurrection, God has made our bodies, His temple, the place where the Holy Spirit resides. What a great honor for the disciple, to be able to enter into worship at any time and place.

The Practice of Worship: Like prayer, worship is indispensable in the life of the believer. Like prayer, worship is best learned by worshipping. Why? It is because ***true*** worship comes from the spirit. That is precisely what Jesus explained to the Samaritan woman that He encountered at the well. He told her, *"True worshippers will worship the Father in spirit and in truth, for they are the kind of worshippers the Father seeks* (John 4:24). Are you the kind of worshipper that the Father is seeking? Is He pleased with your worship because it meets His specification of worship in spirit (from your heart), and in truth (based on accurate knowledge of the Word of God)?

3) THE FUNDAMENTAL OF STUDYING THE WORD:

The Word of God is essential if the disciple is to live a life that is pleasing to God. According to 2 Timothy 2:15, a disciple is required to *"Study to show yourself approved by God, a workman who is not ashamed, rightly dividing the Word of Truth."* The disciple must not only read but study the Word as well so that he or she can accurately interpret truth in order to avoid deception. Peter specifically warns that *"false teachers will secretly introduce false heresies and **many** will follow them"* (2 Pet. 2:1-2). True disciples will not fall into that trap and be easily led astray by the deceptive strategies of the enemy if they know the Word and apply it in their daily lives.

The Practice of Studying the Word: These are 7 simple strategies for studying the Word per Dunnigan and Dennery (2018).

1. **Study Prayerfully** by praying for spiritual insight (Ps. 119:18). from the Holy Spirit who is your ultimate teacher (John 14:26).
2. **Study Carefully:** Since words convey meaning that is essential to understanding the text, look up the meaning of keywords, using Strong's Concordance online at www.blueletterbible.org
3. **Study Repeatedly**: Read the text that you are studying, repeatedly, 4 or more times in different versions. The versions recommended to use for reading are KJV, NKJV, NASB, and NLT.

4. **Study Contextually:** *Near contexts* are the verses and chapters that come before and after the passage under study. *Remote contexts* are other passages on the topic under study. Since the Bible cannot contradict itself, it is crucial to study both near and remote contexts to ensure that your interpretation of the text is consistent throughout Scripture.

5. **Study Realistically:** Put yourself in the middle of the action, become one of the characters, and imagine what it would be like if it was you in that situation. Would you act differently? If so, why and how?

6. **Study Questioningly:** Like any good reporter, ask questions *of* the text – Who? What? When? Where? Why? How? – and then seek the answers *from* the text. You'll be pleasantly surprised at the wealth of knowledge you discover from those answers.

7. **Record Your Observations** that you gleaned from the Holy Spirit. Do your own study **first**, and then check a commentary to see how your insights compare. If different, analyze the reason why and make adjustment in interpretation as needed.

The bottom line is this. Study and knowledge of the Word alone is not sufficient. It is obeying, putting the Word that you studied into practice that is a shield against the deceptive voice of the enemy.

4) THE FUNDAMENTAL OF STEWARDSHIP:

A steward is a person who manages the resources of another. As a steward of God, this is what He requires.

*Each of you should use whatever gift you have received to serve others as **faithful stewards*** (I Peter 4:10).

All that God has given to you, including your gifts, are to be used for God by serving others. Therefore, God's command is, *"Freely you have received, freely give"* (Matt. 10:8): give of yourself, give your time, give your talent, give your treasure! Ultimately, as a steward, you will have to give an account to God for how well you managed all that He has entrusted to you.

The Practice of Stewardship: How one engages in giving is key. Based on scripture, the following are the guidelines forgiving.

1. **Give Generously**: *Give, and it will be given to you. A good measure, pressed down, shaken together and running over, will be poured into your lap* (Luke 6:38).
2. **Give Willingly**: *Give what you have decided in your heart to give* (2 Cor. 9:7). True giving comes from the heart.
3. **Give Joyfully**: *God loves a cheerful giver* (2 Cor. 9:7). Joyful giving is more than a smile; it originates in the heart.
4. **Give Confidently**: *God will supply all your needs according to His riches* (Phil. 4:19). Confidence in giving comes from knowing that He cares and is our loving Provider!
5. **Give Sacrificially**: *The rich gave large amounts out of their wealth, but the widow, out of her poverty, gave more than them because she gave all that she had* (Mark 12:41-44).

Giving that pleases God comes from a heart of love for God and for those whom you serve. That quality of love compels you to obey God's voice. Jesus said it this way. If you love me, keep my commandments (i.e. obey Me). When you give according to God's standards, you are obeying God and rejecting Satan because:

> *No one can serve two masters. Either you will hate the one and love the other, or you will be devoted to the one and despise the other* (Matt. 6:24).

Obedience means you win, God wins, and Satan loses. Only one question remains. Does your giving meet God's standard? Do you give from a heart of love as a disciple of Christ, acting in obedience to His voice? The choice is yours. The choice is always yours. What will you do?

5) THE FUNDAMENTAL OF EVANGELISM:

Evangelism is the spreading of the gospel. It is the means by which the plan of salvation is made known. *"For God is not willing that any should perish, but that all should repent"* (2 Peter 3:9, KJV). Evangelism, making disciples, is indeed the purpose of the church.

The Practice of Evangelism: Dunnigan and Dennery (2018) gives us a simple method for evangelism that uses the acronym R.E.A.P. which stands for: **R**elatable, **E**nthusiastic, **A**ware, **P**repared.
1. **Be Relatable** to those you share the gospel with; not acting as if you are better than they are because you are saved and they are not.
2. **Be Enthusiastic:** Let the joy of the Lord shine in and through you as you share the love of Jesus with others.
3. **Be Aware** of the needs of the person to whom you are speaking. It is difficult for someone to hear the gospel if they are hungry, thirsty, tired, and cold, etc.
4. **Be Prepared**: Always be prepared to evangelize by doing the following three things: a) **Be Prayed Up**. It is the work of the Spirit to prepare the heart of the unsaved and to convict of sin. b) **Be Knowledgeable**. Know the Scriptures, especially those about salvation and how to effectively lead someone to Christ. c) **Be Ready** to share your personal testimony. Your testimony, what God did for you, is irrefutable.

The bottom line is to be a living witness of the gospel by your everyday lifestyle. *Let your light so shine, that they may **see your good deeds** and glorify your Father in heaven* (Matthew 5:16).

Quality time spent in the discipleship activities of prayer, worship and study of the Word develops a strong relationship with Christ so that you hear and obey His voice. That leads to a lifestyle of evangelism combined with stewardship that will diminish the voice of the enemy because your *focus*, your *time* and your *attention* is on pleasing God and serving others.

CHAPTER 14

THE ARMOR OF THE WARRIOR

We dress based on the occasion. If it's a football game, jeans and a jersey is appropriate, but that is not proper dress for a formal party. Likewise, a soldier going to battle would be out of order dressed in a tuxedo or a ballroom gown. Like it or not, as disciples of Christ, we too are soldiers in a battle. Therefore, we must be properly dressed in battle armor so that we not only fight skillfully, but we are victorious over the enemy.

The Commander's Orders:
The order of the Commander-in-Chief, Jesus Christ is simple and to the point. First, He tells us what to do, and then states the reason why. *"Put on the full armor of God, so that you can take your stand against the devil's schemes"* (Eph. 6:11).

The Requirement: It is to put on the full armor of God. Notice that it is the soldier's responsibility to *put on*, to get dressed in the full armor. Two things stand out about this command.
1. God will <u>not</u> dress you. It is totally up to you. Usually, a command given to a soldier is carried out with a "Yes Sir" and a salute. But in this case, the decision is left up to you
2. You must dress in the *full* armor. As a warrior, partial armor is not sufficient to stand against the schemes of the devil.

The Reason: The command is given *"so that you can take your stand against the devil's schemes."* Yes, the devil already has a plan in place. He has schemed and strategized against you. The way to stand firm against his attack is to be *fully* dressed in the armor. But notice, it is not your armor. It is the armor of God, the armor that God has provided for you, but it is your responsibility to put on the *full* armor so that you are prepared for battle.

The Soldier's Duty:

Acquiring the Full Armor: God has provided the full armor that the warrior needs in Ephesians 6:14-18.

> *Stand firm then, with the belt of truth buckled around your waist, with the breastplate of righteousness in place, and with your feet fitted with the readiness that comes from the gospel of peace. In addition to all this, take up the shield of faith, with which you can extinguish all the flaming arrows of the evil one. Take the helmet of salvation and the sword of the Spirit, which is the Word of God.*

Dressing in the Full Armor: The full armor is laid out in the text: 1) the belt of truth, 2) the breastplate of righteousness, 3) feet fitted with the gospel, 4) the shield of faith, 5) the helmet of salvation, and 6) the sword of the Spirit. Now that you know what the armor is, the next step is to do what the Commander says and put it on.

1. **Belt of Truth**: Before a Roman soldier put on his armor, he put a belt around his waist that held up his long robe so that he could move quickly and not easily trip. For the Christian warrior, Jesus is Truth. We know this from John 14:6 that Jesus said, *"I am the Way, the Truth and the Life."* So the belt is the truth that sets you free so that you can move quickly on the battlefield of life and not *trip up* on the lies of the enemy (Olson, 2014). The sword hung in a strap on the belt of truth. It is appropriate that the sword, which represents the Word is also attached to the belt which represents truth. The Word of God is the truth that the believer can have confidence in.

92

2. **Breastplate of Righteousness**: The breastplate protected the heart and lungs of the soldier. In a like fashion, the breastplate that you put on is the fact that you have been made right before God. Therefore, when the enemy attacks with guilt and shame, accusing you before the Father, you can declare that you have been made the righteousness of God through Christ, and instead of retreating, you can boldly advance forward, your heart protected with the knowledge that your sins are forgiven.

3. **Good News Shoes**: Soldiers wore lightweight leather sandals so they could move quickly and with agility for long distances. As warriors for Christ, our feet are fitted with the readiness that comes from the gospel of peace. In other words, we are always on the ready to go and share the gospel that through Christ, both peace with God and the peace of God are available. And for those who already have peace with God, the shoes represent readiness to go and do the will of God. The fervor and focused direction is so strong that if Satan dares to get in the way, he will likely get run over by those gospel shoes.

4. **Shield of Faith**: The Roman shield was held to deflect any arrows that were meant to harm or hurt the soldier. The shield that we hold to protect us against the flaming arrows shot at us by Satan is our faith. His goal is to destroy, but we can block his attempts with the powerful shield of faith in our God.

5. **Helmet of Salvation**: Obviously, the helmet was to protect the head of the soldier. For us, the helmet of salvation is the knowledge that, as believers, we have been saved from our sin and adopted into the family of God. Therefore, when Satan attacks you with negative thoughts, you can boldly counter with the declaration of who you are in Christ... a child of God, a royal priesthood, called out of darkness into the marvelous light of God, freed from the power and penalty of sin.

6. **Sword of the Spirit**: The sword is the only offensive weapon that the soldier carries. All the other pieces of the armor are defensive. For the believer, the sword of the Spirit, which is the Word of God, is the most powerful weapon. Through the Word, Jesus overcame Satan's temptation in the desert, and you can use the Word to overcome Satan as well. Additionally, through His Word comes the power to operate in all the other pieces of armor that He provides... truth, righteousness, peace, faith, and salvation.

Winning With the Armor: When you put on the full armor of God...

    a. His *truth* that sets you free
    b. His *righteousness* that covers you
    c. His *peace* that enables you to share the gospel
    d. His *faith* that shields you from the enemy's attack
    e. His *salvation* that guards against negative thoughts, and
    f. His *Word* to overcome Satan's temptation

...then *"no weapon that the enemy forms against you will prosper"* (Isaiah 54:17). The choice is yours. Will you clothe yourself in the full armor daily so that you can not only fight, but WIN! It's up to you!

PART THREE
THE PRIZE

APPLYING THE VOICE OF TRUTH

THE PRIZE FOR THE FIGHTER
YOUR FREEDOM

OVERVIEW OF PART THREE
THE PRIZE

Whenever a person runs a race, or engages in a boxing match, there is a winner and that person wins a prize. The same is true in the spiritual. When the enemy attacks and you engage him in battle by applying the spiritual strategies discussed in part two consistently and persistently, you are a winner and qualify to obtain a prize. Part of that prize you obtain here and now. That prize is to be set free to live a victorious life as an overcomer, and to live life more abundantly. The other part of the prize will be awarded in the future when Jesus gives the greatest commendation anyone can ever receive, *"Well done, good and faithful servant."*

CHAPTER 15

APPLYING THE VOICE OF TRUTH

Jesus is the voice of Truth. He boldly declares, *"I am the Way, **the Truth** and the Life"* (John 14:6). Jesus speaks the truth, the whole truth and nothing but the truth because He IS truth! When you listen to His voice you can be *certain* that you are hearing the voice of truth. But it is not enough to hear the truth. You must apply the truth to your life in order to receive its benefits.

Using Your Voice to Apply Truth:
In the Garden, Adam's voice was silent, and consequently Eve was deceived. If you are to apply truth to your life, you cannot afford for your voice to be silent.

Use Your Voice To:
1. **Invite Christ into Your Life**. The first thing any person must do to apply the voice of truth is to invite Christ into your life. Your life actually starts when you recognize that you are a sinner and that Jesus Christ is your only hope for salvation.

    *If you **declare** with your mouth, 'Jesus is Lord,' and believe in your heart that God raised him from the dead, you will be saved. For it is with your heart that you believe... and it is with your mouth that you **profess** your faith and are saved* (Rom. 10:9-10).

Applying the Voice of Truth

You must use your voice to apply Romans 10:9-10 in order to have everlasting life according to the truth of John 3:16. You must use your voice to express that you believe that Jesus is the Savior, and Lord of your life.

Use Your Voice To:
2. **Hide the Truth in Your Heart**. After accepting Christ, the next step in applying truth is to "*hide*," literally *place* the truth in your heart and mind. How do you accomplish this? By using your voice as explained in Joshua 1:8.

> *Keep this Book of the Law* [the Word] *always on your* **lips; meditate** *on it day and night, so that you may be careful* **to do** *everything written in it*

The process is simple. The way to keep the Word on your lips is to speak the truth of God's Word by reading it aloud. And then meditate or think about the Word that you read so that it is uppermost in your mind. If you do this consistently, day and night, then the Word will remain in *your heart*, and constantly on *your mind*. That indwelling Word will result in action based on Proverbs 23:7. *As a person thinks, that's what he or she will do*. That is the key for applying the voice of truth to your life.

3. **Call on the Name of Jesus**. There is power in the Name of Jesus, and He has given us the authority to use His Name in prayer. We pray to the Father in the mighty Name of Jesus where we find *help* (2 Chron. 32:8), *hope* (Ps. 39:7), and *healing* (Ps. 30:2). Prayer, talking to the Father, in essence is a declaration of dependence on God for the power to help us win the battle against the tactics of the Second Voice, whose goal is to get us to doubt, deny and disobey God's voice. That Name is so powerful that Philippians 2:10-11 tells us.

> *At the Name of Jesus, every knee should bow, in heaven and on earth and under the earth, and every tongue confesses that Jesus Christ is Lord to the glory of God the Father.*

98

Use Your Voice To:

4. **Influence Others for Good**. In the Garden, Adam's main problem was that he remained silent when he should have used his voice of authority to expel the serpent from the Garden. However, Eve also had an issue with how she used her voice. She used the influence that she had over her husband to get him to eat the fruit and disobey God. Eve did the exact opposite of applying the voice of truth. She swallowed the lie of the enemy and got Adam to do the same. If we are to properly apply the voice of truth, then we must be careful with our words. It is imperative that our words are in agreement with the truth so that we use our influence and advice for good rather than evil.

That is exactly what Joshua did when the people of Israel had to make a decision. As a leader, he took a bold stand for truth.
Joshua assembled all the tribes of Israel at Shechem. He summoned the elders, leaders, judges and officials of Israel... This is what the Lord, the God of Israel, says... I gave you a land on which you did not toil and cities you did not build; and you live in them and eat from vineyards and olive groves that you did not plant.'
Now fear the Lord. Serve him faithfully. Throw away the gods your ancestors worshiped... in Egypt, and serve the Lord. But if serving the Lord seems undesirable to you, then choose for yourselves this day whom you will serve, whether the gods your ancestors served... or the gods of the Amorites, in whose land you are living. But as for me and my household, we will serve the Lord... The people answered, We will serve the Lord and obey Him (Joshua 24:1-2, 13-15, 24).

Joshua demonstrates what it sounds like to apply the voice of truth, to stand for truth and to influence others in the way of truth. How do you use your voice? Do you stand firm footed like Joshua and declare the truth with love and boldness?

Secondly, how do you respond to those who would try to influence you to go in a direction opposite to the Word of God? Do you stand up and lift up your voice for truth. We can look to Job for such an example. When Job lost all his wealth, his health, and all 10 of his children, this is how his wife said to him.

Are you still maintaining your integrity? Why don't you curse God and die (Job 2:9)!

That's the kind of advice Eve gave to Adam. But Job does not take his wife's advice, nor does he remain silent. He speaks truth to her error.

You are talking like a foolish woman. Shall we accept good from God, and not trouble? In all this, Job did not sin in what he said (Job 2:9-10).

In short, the Word of Truth is the premiere weapon you have that you can apply in order to resist the strategies of the enemy. That is why the Word is called the *Sword of the Spirit* in Ephesians 6. Without the Word in your head and heart, you are defenseless against Satan's voice. But when armed with the power of the Word, **spoken** by you with a heart filled with faith, you can resist the devil, diminish his deceptive voice, and watch him run away from you.

CHAPTER 16

THE PRIZE FOR THE FIGHTER:
YOUR FREEDOM

When you know the truth and then apply that truth to your life, Jesus said, *"the truth will set you free"* (John 8:32). Merriam Webster defines **free** as:
1. not subject to the control or domination of another
2. choosing or capable of choosing for itself

The definition above makes it clear that there are two components to freedom; one negative, the other positive. First, it is NOT to be under the control or domination of another. In this case, it is not to be dominated by sin and Satan. The Apostle Paul explains it like this in Romans 6:12-14.

__Do not__ let sin reign in your mortal body so that you obey its evil desires. __Do not__ offer any part of yourself to sin as an instrument of wickedness, but rather offer yourselves to God as those who have been brought from death to life; and offer every part of yourself to him as an instrument of righteousness. For __sin shall no longer be your master__ because you are not under the law, but under grace.

There it is! **Freedom is a choice**. It is to choose NOT to allow sin to rule you or to be your master. You accomplish that by knowing the truth (God's Word), and applying the truth to your life through the power of the Holy Spirit.

The truth of God's Word spoken by you which results in living a righteous life sets you free. You are set free...

1. from the bondage of sin
2. to hear and heed the voice of the Shepherd
3. to use the powerful Name of Jesus
4. to obtain the prize

It is critical to understand that freedom has to be maintained. Why? Simply because the Second Voice does not quit! Satan may leave for a season, but you can be assured that he will return, and like a good soldier, you must be on guard, vigilant, battle-ready, dressed in the full armor of God, in tune to the voice of your Commander-in-Chief, Jesus Christ.

OBTAINING THE PRIZE:

In order to obtain and maintain the prize, two things are required. You must be disciplined and determined.

Discipline Required: Discipline is required to get and hold on to the prize. In I Corinthians 9:24-27, the great Apostle Paul uses two analogies involving athletes, to help us understand the requirement. He talks first about a runner, and then a boxer.

*Do you not know that in a race all the **runners** run, but only one gets the **prize**? Run in such a way as to get the prize. Everyone who competes in the games goes into **strict training**. They do it to get a crown that will not last, but we do it to get a crown that will last forever. Therefore I do not run like someone running aimlessly.*

*I do not fight like a **boxer** beating the air. No, I strike a blow to my body and make it my slave so that after I have preached to others, I myself will not be disqualified for the **prize**.*

A Marathon: The Christian walk is not a sprint. It is a marathon so you must be prepared for the long haul. Just like a runner or a boxer who wants to win, you must go into strict training.

1. **Dietary Restrictions** – There are certain things an athlete cannot eat, likewise there are certain things a Christian cannot consume. We eat with our ears, eyes, mouths, and bodies. Therefore, there are certain things that a disciplined Christian cannot listen to or look at in order to be in top form to win.
2. **Dietary Requirements** – On the other hand, athletes <u>must</u> eat certain things to build up strength to go long distances. In a similar fashion, believers must feast on the milk and the meat of the Word (Heb. 5:12) so that they can grow in grace and knowledge of Jesus Christ (2 Peter 3:18).
3. **Water Intake** – Water is essential that is why there are water stations along the marathon route. Similarly, Jesus is the Water of Life. We must drink deeply from the water of the Word that He gives us just like He gave the woman at the well (Jn. 4:14).
4. **Exercise** – A runner must exercise to build muscle. We have to develop our spiritual muscles as well through the discipleship activities of prayer, study, worship, giving and evangelism so that we can go the distance.

Are you training consistently and persistently so you can obtain the prize, which is freedom to live the abundant life here and now and everlasting life with the Father, Son, and Holy Spirit? The choice is yours. What will it be?

Determination Required: To be successful at anything, one must be determined to win. That is what Paul did to win the prize.

Not that I have already obtained all this, or have already arrived at my goal, but I <u>press</u> on to take hold of that for which Christ Jesus took hold of me. Brothers and sisters, I do not consider myself yet to have taken hold of it. But one thing I do: Forgetting what is behind and <u>straining</u> toward what is ahead, I press on toward the goal to win the **prize** (Phil. 3:13-14).

Pressing for the Prize: Winning the prize is not easy. It requires effort. According to Paul, you have to press forward to the mark, the goal, the finish line. In doing so, he talks about two things that must be done.

1. Forgetting what is behind
2. Straining toward what is ahead

A NOTE OF HOPE

Failure Is Not Final: Know this, if at any point, you should fail, even with all you know, and have learned from this book, remember that God's love is such that you can always run to Him. Failure is not final or fatal if you run to God who is always ready and willing to forgive, standing with arms wide open to receive and restore you. *"The one who is in you is greater than the one who is in the world"* (I John 4:4). If you fall down, don't stay down. Get up, confess that you missed the mark, receive God's forgiveness and **keep moving forward**.

> *In all these things we are more than conquerors through him who loved us... convinced that neither death nor life, neither angels nor demons, neither the present nor the future, nor any powers, neither height nor depth, nor anything else in all creation, will be able to separate us from the love of God that is in Christ Jesus our Lord.*

Free Indeed: You are indeed FREE. Free to live the abundant life, free to love God and others, free to return to fellowship with God whenever it is necessary. Live in the FREEDOM that Christ has given to you!

BIBLIOGRAPHY

Dennery, C. B. (2009). *Christ and Covenant: Key to the Scripture.* Delaware: Doctrine101 Publishers.

Dunnigan, D.E. & Dennery, C. B. (2018). *Connecting: Key to Dynamic Discipleship.* Delaware: Doctrine101 Publishers.

Krejoir, R.J. (2007). *Statistics and Reasons for Church Decline.* Retrieved from http://www.churchleadership.org/apps/articles/default.asp?articleid=42346

Merriam-Webster online dictionary. Retrieved from https://www.merriam-webster/dictionary.com

Olson, T. (2014). *The Belt of Truth.* Retrieved from https://unlockingthebible.org/2014/03/the-belt-of-truth-part-i/

Shull, K. (2018). *Hope for Dying Churches.* Retrieved from https://factsandtrends.net/2018/01/16/hope-for-dying-churches/

Statistics in the Ministry (2018). Retrieved from https://www.pastoralcareinc.com/statistics/